SEVEN
WHOLE
DAYS

Common dog violet (*Viola riviniana*)

SEVEN WHOLE DAYS

A Christian's Prayer Book

Compiled by
BROTHER KENNETH CGA

Illustrations by
CLARE ROBERTS

MOWBRAY

Mowbray
A Cassell imprint
Villiers House, 41/47 Strand,
London WC2N 5EJ, England

First published 1990

ISBN 0-264-67171-6 (green)
0-264-67200-3 (white)

Typeset by Colset Pte. Ltd., Singapore
Printed and bound in Great Britain by
The Bath Press, Avon

Contents

Abbreviations of Bible translations   vi

List of illustrations   vii

Acknowledgements   viii

Introduction   ix

WORK OF GOD (liturgy prayer)   1

IN A NUTSHELL (Collects)   15

PRIVATE PRAYERS   23

MY GOD AND KING (hymns as prayers)   29

STRING PRAYERS   37
   ARROW PRAYERS   42
   JESUS PRAYER   43
   'CHOPPING' PRAYER   44

WERE YOU THERE? (imaginative prayer)   47

OUR FATHER   55

PRAYERS OF SAINTS — AND SINNERS!   63

PRAYERS OF PREPARATION   83
   FOR SUNDAY   83
   FOR HOLY COMMUNION   84
   FOR MAKING IT UP WITH GOD   89
   FOR MAKING IT UP WITH A FRIEND   92
   FOR EXAMS   93
   FOR STARTING SOMETHING NEW   93

THANKSGIVING AND PRAISE   95
   FOR HOLY COMMUNION   95

CONTENTS

GENERAL THANKSGIVINGS | 98
IN PRAISE OF CHRIST | 101
FOR SAINTS | 102
FOR LIFE AND FAITH | 103

PRAYERS FOR OTHERS — AND MYSELF | 105
FOR OTHER PEOPLE | 105
PERSONAL PRAYERS | 112

LORD HEAR US | 117
LITANY OF CHRIST IN GLORY | 118
LITANY OF THE CHURCH IN THE WORLD | 119
LITANY OF THE HOLY SPIRIT | 120
LITANY OF THE TRINITY | 121
LITANY FOR PEACE | 122
LITANY OF GETHSEMANE | 126
NIGHT LITANY | 128

Index of Subjects | 131

Index of Selected Lines | 134

Index of Sources | 137

Bibliography | 145

Abbreviations of Bible translations

JB   The Jerusalem Bible

NEB   The New English Bible

RSV   The Revised Standard Version

TEV   Good News Bible: Today's English Version

Illustrations

Woodruff *(Galium odoratum)*   *front cover*

Common dog violet *(Viola riviniana)*   *frontispiece*

Dog roses *(Rosa canina)*   xiv

Yellow flag iris *(Iris pseudacorus)*   14

Turfmoss *(Sphagnum sp.)* with wood sorrel *(Oxalis acetosella)*   22

Hart's tongue fern *(Phyllitis scolopendrium)* with herb Robert *(Geranium robertianum)*   28

Marsh marigold *(Caltha palustris)*   36

Pussy willow *(Salix caprea)*   46

Wild strawberry *(Fragaria vesca)*   54

Blackcap nest *(Sylvia atricapilla)*   62

Field bindweed *(Convolvulus arvensis)*   82

Cowslip *(Primula veris)*   94

Greater celandine *(Chelidonium majus)*   104

Fronds of male fern *(Dryopteris filix-mas)*   116

Lady's mantle *(Alchemilla mollis)*   130

The illustrations are by Clare Roberts, who has taught at the Bourne-mouth and Poole College of Art and Design, was the illustrator of God's Acre, and has held a number of exhibitions of her work including an exhibition of drawings and watercolours at the Wigmore Hall.

Acknowledgements

The compiler and publishers are grateful for permission to quote from the following:

Good News Bible © American Bible Society 1976, published by the Bible Societies and Collins

Jerusalem Bible, published and copyright © 1966, 1967 and 1968 by Darton, Longman & Todd Ltd, and Doubleday, a division of Bantam, Doubleday, Dell Publishing Group, Inc.

New English Bible second edition, © 1970 Oxford and Cambridge University Presses

Revised Standard Version © National Council of the Churches of Christ in the USA

Extracts from the *Book of Common Prayer* of 1662, the rights of which are vested in the Crown in perpetuity within the United Kingdom, reproduced by permission of Eyre & Spottiswoode Publishers, Her Majesty's Printers, London

Prayers for a Lifetime by Karl Rahner, published by T. & T. Clark Ltd

'Solzhenitsyn's Prayer,' published by Keston College in *Religion in Communist Lands*, vol. 2, no. 2 (March/April 1974)

Gitanjali by Rabindranath Tagore, published 1913 by Macmillan & Co. Ltd

Manual of Prayers for War Time by William Temple, published 1939 by A. R. Mowbray & Co. Ltd

Version of the Lord's Prayer based on the interpretation given by Karl Barth according to the Reformers, included in *Prayer and Preaching*, published 1964 by SCM Press

Brother Roger of Taizé, in *The Letter from Taizé*

Night Litany: Community of the Sisters of the Church

Read this–it's important

Did you buy this book for yourself, or was it a present? Perhaps it celebrates your birthday, Christmas, Easter? Or your Confirmation, First Communion or admission to full membership of your church? The trouble with presents, especially books, however well intentioned, is that they might not be to your taste. In the case of a book of prayers, for instance, it rather depends too on how you and God get on. Not, you will understand, how God is getting on with you. About that there is no question: he loves you, just as you are. Our love for him is sometimes the problem. Prayer books, if they are properly used, are a way to help us solve it.

A prayer book or a book about prayer—and in a fairly simple way this tries to be both—is not the kind of reading matter which you begin at page one and just plough through until you come to the end. To do that, though, with this one before you actually attempt to pray with it might not be such a bad idea. At least if you do read it through you will discover exactly what is in it. You might also come across a prayer that you've always liked whenever you have heard it, but up till now have not had the slightest idea where it came from. And let's be honest, you'll also discover some prayers or ideas that you don't like or couldn't possibly use.

If this were a cookery book you would now be ready for the kitchen, but where is the best place to pray? And when? Let's consider place first. It varies, as you would expect, depending on each person but it does help to find somewhere quiet—warm too, if the weather is cold; a place where you can sit on a chair, or cross-legged on the floor, kneel or stand as you wish, and perhaps a place where you can, if you want to, pray aloud. If you have a room of your own, no problem; but if you share a bedroom choose a time a time when you can have it to yourself.

It is a good idea to organise our prayer life in exactly the same way as we organise our social or working lives, or even our sports training routines. It is true that for many of us prayer comes more easily in the morning rather than later in the day or just before we go to bed, and for someone like me, a member of a religious community, it is simple to pray in the morning because life is geared to that sort of thing. However, for others early morning is more difficult. Only *you* can decide which is the best time for you. When you have decided, unless you are reviewing your whole life, which ought not to happen every day, stick to it.

You've decided when you are going to pray each day (you might well have chosen different times for Saturdays and Sundays); now you have to make up your mind for how long. Five minutes? Seven minutes? Ten minutes? A quarter of an hour . . .? Do not be over-ambitious. Choose a length of time you know you will have no excuse for cutting short, and when you have chosen keep to it. Even when you have run out of ideas or words stay put, wherever you choose to pray, until the time you have decided to offer to God has been completed.

The first seven chapters set out seven different ways of praying, so that you could, if you wanted use each chapter at the rate of one a day, as the basis of your prayer for a week. In that way you would begin to discover which methods of prayer suit you best. The seven sections, by the way, do not represent the only ways into prayer, but doubtless you'd taken that as read.

If you find any section particularly difficult don't give up on it immediately. Try it again in a few weeks' time to check that it wasn't just a bad day when you tried that method. If it doesn't work a second time put it on one side and try again a third time later on; and if you still can't get on with it you will know that it is not for you, at least for the time being. We are all different so don't be surprised to discover you can make more sense of one method than another.

You have already had to learn how to walk; to talk; to read; to write; to swim, perhaps; to ride a bicycle and a thousand other activities since you first came into the world. Praying is another human activity which initially has to be learned as well.

Over the centuries book after book has been written to explain how to pray, or to exhort God's children to pray. As there are experts in nuclear physics or neuro-surgery so there are experts in prayer. I am not an expert, simply one who tries to make easily available some of the prayer-knowledge that is around.

The section entitled 'Prayers of Saints and Sinners' contains a comprehensive collection of prayers from the first to the present century. If you want to find a prayer by a particular person, look him or her up in the index of sources. If you are familiar with the first line of a prayer but cannot recall the rest of it, there is an index of lines as well. The titles of the other sections are, I hope, self-explanatory.

Many, if not most of the ideas come from other people, way back to the beginning of the Church. At the end of each prayer is given its source—where known—the name of the person who has inspired or written (or partly written) it. The actual words, however, are rarely exactly as they left the author's pen. I have not scrupled to alter and adapt or leave out passages where I thought it made the meaning clearer, or the prayer easier to use. For a more purist approach look at the *Oxford Book of Prayer*! Prayers that have no indication of source are mine.

Prayer is not always easy. There will be occasions when you don't feel in the mood. Those are times when it would be safer to stick closely to whatever book you are using. There will be other times when you feel cut off from God, probably through your own fault, and you will be tempted to skip your prayer time. Those are the times when you need to pray the more fervently. There will also be times when prayer is so important that you'll find no difficulty in giving your time to God. However you feel, do remember that your moods are not the most important aspect of your being. Prayer is one of the ways in which we show God our love. After all it would be pretty strange to assure your friend that you loved her or him and then deliberately refuse to speak for days on end. Your friend might just begin to wonder. . . . Mercifully God does not cease to love us when we treat him badly. He doesn't even fall out with us as quickly as we fall out with him.

Apart from those times when we meet with our fellow Christians for worship, prayer can feel as though it is something we do on our own. Finding a quiet place where we can be alone to pray emphasises the fact, and yet alone is what we are not! We never pray alone. Prayer and praise are the constant activity of Heaven. When we pray we are, as it were, plugging in to the praise and worship of all the angels and saints. St Paul assures us that it is 'by the Spirit's power we cry out to God' (Romans 8.15). United to the whole company of heaven, with Christians who have loved and served God through the ages, and in the power of the Holy Spirit, we pour out our hearts to God our Father in the name of his son Jesus, for we too are the children of God.

Go to it, and God bless you.

KENNETH CGA
Feast of SS Timothy and Titus, 1989

Dog roses (*Rosa canina*)

Work of God

The first Christians, obviously, were nearly all Jews; familiar like Jesus with worship in the synagogues. Specifically Christian services developed out of this Jewish worship and consisted of psalms, readings from the Bible and prayers. St Benedict, founder of Western monasticism, called his brothers' seven daily services (or 'Offices') the 'Work of God'. And it is work not just meant for monks and nuns. Priests in parishes say their Office every day, usually by themselves, though sometimes others come to pray with them. When we pray an Office we are consciously drawing on the riches of the Church's liturgy and linking our prayers with those being offered the whole world over. Not only that, the psalms, which form the basis of the 'Work of God', have been hallowed with the breath of Jesus himself so that, though all Christian prayer is offered in his name, the Office is in a special way the prayer of Christ.

Read your Office slowly. You might find it helpful to read it aloud—if you can cope with the embarrassment! After all, in mediaeval times silent reading was the more unusual.

A prayer to say before you begin:

Father in heaven,
By the power of your Holy Spirit,
purify me from being too wrapped up in myself;
keep my mind from wandering,
and my thoughts pure.
Help me to understand what I read,
and let it deepen my love for you,
that in union with your Son,
Jesus Christ,
and your people everywhere,
I may add my praises
to the prayers of your angels and saints
in the glory of heaven.

1

O God make speed to save me: come quickly to my help.

Glory to the Father, and to the Son and to the Holy Spirit as
   it was in the beginning, is now, and shall be for ever. Amen.

Alleluia!

In the morning say the Jubilate *(Psalm 100):*

Be joyful in the Lord all nations: serve the Lord with gladness
   and come into his presence with a song.
Know the Lord, the God who made us: we are his people and
   the sheep of his flock.
Enter his gates with thanksgiving, and into his courts with
   praise: be thankful to him and speak good of his name.
For the Lord is good, his love is everlasting: his constancy
   endures from generation to generation.
Glory to the Father, and to the Son and to the Holy Spirit: as
   it was in the beginning, is now and shall be for ever.
   Amen.

In the evening say the Phos hilaron *(a very ancient Greek
hymn):*

Jesus Christ,
Gladsome Light!
From the glory of the Father
Gleaming.
Life and Light
Is your gift to the world.

Day is gone;
Night has come;
But night and day I want to praise
My God.

For the glory of the Son,
Holy heavenly blessed One,
Shines through all the world.

*Now the hymn. (If you want a change from this one use a poem
from pages 30–35, 76, or perhaps the 'Canticle of Brother Sun'
on pages 69f.)*

King of glory, King of peace
   I will love thee:
And that love may never cease,
   I will move thee.
Thou hast granted my request,
   Thou hast heard me;
Thou didst note my working breast,
   Thou hast spared me.

Wherefore with my utmost art
   I will sing thee.
And the cream of all my heart
   I will bring thee.
Though my sins against me cried,
   Thou didst clear me;
And alone when they replied,
   Thou didst hear me.

Seven whole days, not one in seven,
   I will praise thee;
In my heart, though not in heaven
   I can raise thee.
Small it is, in this poor sort
   To enroll thee;
E'en eternity's too short
   To extol thee.

GEORGE HERBERT

3

*A psalm, or psalms, follow. It is probably a good idea some-
times to say more than one. When you read them, silently or
aloud, always pause at the colon which divides each verse.*

Psalm 33.3–12

Sing to the Lord a new song: play loudly with all your skill;
For the word of the Lord holds true: and all his works are
faithful.
The Lord loves righteousness and justice: the earth is full of
his goodness;
By the word of the Lord were the heavens made: by the
breath of his mouth all the stars.
He gathered the waters of the sea: the depths he stores in his
treasures.
Let all the earth fear the Lord: stand in awe of him you that
live in the world.
For he spoke and it was done: he commanded and it sprang
into being.
The Lord brings the plans of nations to nothing: he frustrates
the intentions of the peoples.
The Lord's own plans shall stand for ever: the intentions of
his heart for all generations.
Happy the nation whose God is the Lord: the people he has
chosen for his own possession.
Glory to the Father and to the Son and to the Holy Spirit: as
it was in the beginning, is now, and shall be for ever.
Amen.

Psalm 42.1–5

As a deer longs for running streams: so do I long for you, O
God.
With my whole being I thirst for God: the God of my life.
When shall I come to God: and appear in his presence?
My tears have been my bread day and night: 'Where is your
God?' they ask me all day long.

I remember and my soul melts within me: how I went to the
  house of God.
Amid cries of gladness and thanksgiving: an exultant throng.
Why are you so downcast my soul: groaning in distress?
Put your hope in God: for I shall praise him yet, my saviour
  and my God.
Glory to the Father and to the Son and to the Holy Spirit: as
  it was in the beginning, is now, and shall be for ever.
  Amen.

Psalm 98.1–6

Sing a new song to the Lord: for he has done marvellous
  things.
His right hand and his holy arm: have gained him the
  victory.
The Lord has displayed his power: and revealed his justice to
  the nations;
Mindful of his love and faithfulness: to the house of Israel.
All the ends of the world have seen: the salvation of our God.
Acclaim the Lord all who live on the earth: sing, rejoice and
  give thanks.
O show yourselves joyful: before the Lord our King.
Glory to the Father and to the Son and to the Holy Spirit: as
  it was in the beginning, is now, and shall be for ever.
  Amen.

Psalm 103.1–3, 9, 11–13

Praise the Lord O my soul: and all that is within me praise
  his holy name.
Praise the Lord O my soul: and remember all his kindnesses,
In forgiving all your sins: and healing all your suffering.
He will not always be chiding: or nurse his anger for ever.
For as the heaven stands high above the earth: so his strong
  love stands high over all who fear him.

Look how far the east is from the west: so far has he put all
   our offences from us.
As tenderly as a father treats his children: so has the Lord
   compassion on all who fear him.
Glory to the Father and to the Son and to the Holy Spirit: as
   it was in the beginning, is now, and shall be for ever.
   Amen.

Psalm 150

Praise God in his holiness: praise him in his temple in heaven;
Praise him for his mighty works: praise him for his
   immeasurable greatness!
Praise him with the blasts of the trumpet: praise him upon
   lute and harp;
Praise him with drums and dancing: praise him upon flute
   and strings;
Praise him with the clash of cymbals: praise him upon
   clanging cymbals;
Let everything that has breath: praise the Lord; Alleluia!
Glory to the Father and to the Son and to the Holy Spirit: as
   it was in the beginning, is now and shall be for ever.
   Amen.

*After the psalmody, read a lesson. There is no need to stick to
those printed below if you have your Bible handy.*

Mark 1.32–38 (NEB)

That evening after sunset they brought to Jesus all who were ill
or possessed by devils; and the whole town was there, gathered
at the door. He healed many who suffered from various
diseases, and drove out many devils. He would not let the devils
speak, because they knew who he was.

   Very early next morning he got up and went out. He went
away to a lonely spot and remained there in prayer. But Simon
and his companions searched him out, found him, and said,

'They are all looking for you.' He answered, 'Let us move on to the country towns in the neighbourhood; I have to proclaim my message there also; that is that I came out to do.'

Luke 6.27–31 (TEV)

Jesus said, 'I tell you who hear me: Love your enemies, do good to those who hate you, bless those who curse you, and pray for those who ill-treat you. If anyone hits you on one cheek, let him hit the other one too; if someone takes your coat, let him have your shirt as well. Give to everyone who asks you for something, and when someone takes what is yours, do not ask for it back. Do for others just what you want them to do for you.'

Ephesians 3.14–19 (NEB)

With this in mind, then, I kneel in prayer to the Father, from whom every family in heaven and on earth takes its name, that out of the treasures of his glory he may grant you strength and power through his Spirit in your inner being, that through faith Christ may dwell in your hearts in love. With deep roots and firm foundations, may you be strong to grasp, with all God's people, what is the breadth and length and height and depth of the love of Christ, and know it, though it is beyond knowledge. So may you attain to fullness of being, the fullness of God himself.

1 Timothy 3.16 (JB)

Without any doubt, the mystery of our religion is very deep indeed:

> He was made visible in the flesh,
> attested by the Spirit,
> seen by angels,
> proclaimed to the pagans,
> believed in by the world,
> taken up in glory.

Now for the prayers. The first one is often repeated three times. It is called the Trisagion, *which means 'Thrice holy'. When you've said it the reason for the name is fairly obvious!*

Holy God,
Holy and strong
Holy and immortal one
Have mercy on us.

The Lord's Prayer follows (use whichever version you like best).

Our Father in heaven,
hallowed be your name,
your kingdom come,
your will be done,
on earth as in heaven.
Give us today our daily bread.
Forgive us our sins
as we forgive those who sin against us.
Lead us not into temptation
but deliver us from evil.

For the kingdom, the power, and the glory are yours
now and for ever. Amen.

Our Father, who art in heaven,
hallowed be thy name;
thy kingdom come;
thy will be done
on earth as it is in heaven.
Give us this day our daily bread.
And forgive us our trespasses,
as we forgive those who trespass against us.
And lead us not into temptation;
but deliver us from evil.

For thine is the kingdom, the power, and the glory,
for ever and ever. Amen.

Hail Mary, full of grace, the Lord is with thee. Blessed art
thou among women, and blessed is the fruit of thy womb,
Jesus.
Holy Mary, Mother of God, pray for us sinners, now and at
the hour of our death. Amen.

In the morning, use one or two of the following prayers.

O Holy Trinity, one God, to you I humbly offer my soul and
body, my thoughts and ideas, my words and my actions, my
hopes and my fears, my heart and all its affections: all that I
have and all that I am, to be governed, guided and sanctified
by you this day and evermore. Amen.

ANON

Almighty God, maker of everything in heaven and earth. You
are good and do good continually. Thank you for taking care
of me so that I am alive and well this morning. Save me, O
God, from evil today and let me love and serve you for ever,
for the sake of your Son Jesus Christ. Amen.

ISAAC WATTS

Give me, O God, the highest learning to know you; and the
best wisdom to know myself. Bless my studies that I may
learn what will be for my good. Let me be wholly given to
your service and let me count all things as so much rubbish
when compared to the knowledge of Christ Jesus my Lord to
whom with you and the Holy Spirit be all honour and glory
for ever and ever. Amen.

JOHN WESLEY

Lord God Almighty, thank you for having preserved me
through the past night, and for granting me health and
strength for today. I bless you for all your mercies: for giving
me food to eat, clothes to put on, and for delivering me from
many evils. I thank you especially for the gift of Jesus Christ.

For his sake grant me the help of your Holy Spirit, that I may
be able to follow my Saviour's example and do whatever he
commands. May I be patient, humble, kind and merciful,
forgiving those who sin against me, even as I hope to be
forgiven. Grant me grace to do what I have to do diligently
and to be true and just in all my dealings. Help me, Lord, to
restrain my tongue and keep my temper. Save me from those
sins which in the past most easily have defeated me;
strengthen me for all that awaits me; carry me through all my
troubles, and help me, day by day, to grow in grace, and in
the knowledge of my Lord and Saviour, Jesus Christ. Amen.

HANNAH MORE

Thanks be to God,
Who brought me from yesterday
To the beginning of today;
Everlasting joy to earn for my soul.

Thanks be to God,
Who wants my good;
Who gives me peace.

My thoughts, my words,
My deeds, my desires,
I dedicate to you;
And I ask you most humbly
To keep me from offence;
Shield me tonight,
For the sake of your wounds,
And your gift of grace.

ALEX CARMICHAEL
(translated from the Gaelic)

*In the evening, use one or two of these prayers. (If you want a
change you could use one of the litanies between pages 118 and
129.)*

Whatever is happening in this world, Lord, may I always seek first your glory. May your splendour fill me with light, far beyond the splendour of sun or moon or shining stars; may I appreciate the beauty of your kingdom as revealed in the gospel and see the brightness of your glory piercing through the darkness and despair of this world towards our eternal inheritance in Christ Jesus our Lord. Amen.

JOHN CALVIN

Great and glorious Majesty, God and Father of our Lord Jesus Christ, who taught *us* to call you Father as well, look from the place of your holiness. You know all that I do and the secrets of my heart. How shall a rebel lift up a guilty face? If it was only today's sins! But too often have I forgotten you. I beg forgiveness through Jesus my Saviour. Remove all evil from me. Let your Spirit renew me, and make me holy as you are holy that I may grow daily more able to do what is right and enjoy the blessedness of your kingdom. Amen.

ISAAC WATTS

Lord, I am so dim; my mind fixed on my own concerns that I cannot respond when you stretch out your hand to me. Let your Holy Spirit rouse me to look up to you, striving against my inner blindness, that I may come to know you as you already know me, and at length arrive at that perfect glory which you have prepared for us in heaven, through Jesus Christ our Lord. Amen.

JOHN CALVIN

May your pity, O God, protect me from all gradual and piecemeal surrenders to my old nature; and make a new and holy life a reality for me through Jesus Christ our Lord. Amen.

Sarum Missal

11

Father, I sometimes feel you are over-indulgent towards my sins. May I be dissatisfied and cut down to size by true sorrow for them. From this moment may I devote myself wholeheartedly to your service and at the end of my life obtain the blessedness which Jesus by his blood has bought for us.

JOHN CALVIN

Watch, dear Lord, with those who cannot sleep and those who weep this night. Tend the sick, give rest to the weary and bless the dying, relieve those who suffer, have pity on those in great distress and keep those who are happy, for your love's sake.

ST AUGUSTINE

Support us O Lord, all the day long of this troublous life, until the shades lengthen, the evening comes, the busy world is hushed, the fever of life is over and our work is done, then Lord in thy mercy, grant us safe lodging, a holy rest and peace at the last, through Jesus Christ our Lord.

JOHN HENRY NEWMAN

Finish your Office with one of the following blessings.

The grace of our Lord Jesus Christ, and the love of God, and the fellowship of the Holy Spirit be with us all evermore. Amen.

May the souls of the faithful, through the mercy of God, rest in peace.

Blessing and honour and thanksgiving and praise, more than we can utter, more than we can conceive, be yours, O holy and glorious Trinity, Father, Son and Holy Spirit, from all angels, all men, all creation for ever and ever. Amen.

To God, who working in us can do so much more than we can ever ask for, or even think of, to him be glory in the

Church and in Christ Jesus, for all time, and for ever and
ever. Amen.

*Now spend at least thirty seconds being quiet—to give God a
chance!*

Yellow flag iris (*Iris pseudacorus*)

In a nutshell

Dame Julian of Norwich, the fourteenth-century anchoress, experienced a series of visions. In one she saw a hand cradling a hazelnut. She perceived it was like the hand of God holding the world and understood that 'God made the world, he loves it and he keeps it'. The prayers in this section are mostly collects, so called because they gather up ideas into short pithy phrases, like Dame Julian's. Another of hers, 'All shall be well, and all shall be well, and all manner of things shall be well', is a source of great comfort, assuring us that whatever happens to us in the world's terms, be it good or bad, God is still in ultimate control.

You'll get spiritual constipation if you use all the following collects at once. They have been divided into three groups in any case; but if a phrase or a word, here or anywhere else in the book, starts ringing bells with you, abandon the printed page and listen to God.

Lord Jesus Christ, son of the living God,
place your passion, cross and death
between your judgement and me,
now and when I come to die.
Of your great love, grant mercy and grace to the living;
rest and glory to the dead;
peace and unity in the church;
and to us sinners, eternal joy and happiness.

J. M. NEALE

Holy Spirit, breathe on me:
purify; enliven; refresh me.
Every day draw closer to me
and me closer to you:
For the sake of Jesus Christ
to whom with you and the Father
be all wonder and delight,
all worship and adoration,
all praise and glory,
now and for ever.

MARK FRANK

Strike, Lord, strike at the root of the poverty of my love for
    you.
Strengthen me to bear both my sorrows and my joys, to
    make my love fruitful in service:
Strengthen me to rise above the trifling aggravations of daily
    life,
and for love to surrender myself to you.

RABINDRANATH TAGORE

Since you so graciously invite us to yourself, Almighty God,
    do not withdraw the invitation however deaf we remain.
Grant that I may be disciplined and open to your word,
obeying you, not just for a single day,

nor yet a few weeks,
but to the end of my life,
for the sake of Jesus Christ our Lord.

JOHN CALVIN

Father, save me from my own will and let your will be done
in me, and by me. As I grow older may I grow also in
wisdom and your favour until you take me to your
everlasting kingdom to reign with you for ever.

JOHN WESLEY

King of righteousness, lead us in the ways of justice and
peace. Inspire us to break down all tyranny and oppression,
that we may gain for everyone a due reward, and ask from
everyone proper service; that each may live for all, and all
may care for each in the name of Jesus the Lord.

WILLIAM TEMPLE

God be in my head, and in my understanding;
God be in my eyes and in my looking;
God be in my mouth and in my speaking;
God be in my head and in my thinking;
God be at my end, and at my departing.

Sarum Primer

And if you are praying in the morning before you go out:

Lord you know how busy I shall be today.
If I forget you, I know you won't forget me.

JACOB ASTLEY

*   *   *

Knowledge about you, Almighty God, ought to be deep-
   rooted in me for you make yourself known,
not only by the law and the prophets,
but also by your only begotten Son.
Grant that I may continue firm and constant in my response
   to you,
striving to extend your kingdom,
not only in my own life,
but in the lives of all who honour the name of Jesus Christ
   our Lord.

JOHN CALVIN

Blessed Jesus, now that you have exalted and sanctified
   human nature and made even my body precious,
help me to treat it reverently not daring to put it to wrong
   use,
that I may live a holy life with you in the world,
and after my death may reign with you in glory.

JEREMY TAYLOR

Lord God, give us a steadfast faith, a living hope and fervent
   love.
Make us humble and prepared to learn,
always kind in whatever we do or say,
truthful and honest,
that having a good conscience both towards you and each
   other,
we may render up our account without fear at the last day,
through Jesus Christ our Lord.

ANON

Accept, O my God, this my sacrifice of praise and thanks:
and since the longer I live the more I experience thy most
adorable and boundless goodness; so the more devoutly may
I daily praise thee and the more intensely may I daily love
thee, through Jesus Christ thy Beloved.

THOMAS KEN

Most tender and gentle Lord Jesus,
when will my heart have some of your perfection?
When will my hard and stony heart,
my proud heart, my unbelieving, my impure heart,
my narrow selfish heart,
be melted and made like yours?
Teach me to think deeply about you,
that I may become like you,
and love you sincerely and simply,
as you love me.

JOHN HENRY NEWMAN

Jesus, grant me so much of your love that I may truly love
my sisters and brothers. Give us a fellow feeling for one
another's calamities, and a readiness to bear each other's
burdens. Teach me when to say nothing and when to offer
advice. Make me aware of the dangers which threaten them,
and help me to rejoice when they rejoice, that together we
may come to your eternal kingdom.

MARK FRANK

Grant, Lord, that in your wounds I may find my safety:
in your pain, my peace;
in your cross, my victory,
in your resurrection, my triumph;
and a crown of righteousness in the glories of your eternal
    kingdom.

JEREMY TAYLOR

*   *   *

19

Father, lover and restorer of innocence, draw to yourself the hearts of your servants that being inflamed with the fire of your spirit, they may be true to their faith and zealous in doing good, through Jesus Christ our Lord.

Sarum Missal

O Almighty God, who alone canst order the unruly wills and affections of sinful men; Grant unto thy people, that they may love the thing which thou commandest, and desire that which thou dost promise; that so, among the sundry and manifold changes of the world, our hearts may surely there be fixed, where true joys are to be found: through Jesus Christ our Lord. Amen.

Book of Common Prayer

May God who helps us and pours his blessings on us
continue to have me and mine under his protection.
May he prosper all our plans to his glory,
and strengthen our hearts against all the power of the enemy,
through Jesus Christ our Lord.

JOHN WESLEY

Lord, give me grace to be generous towards others
and stern with myself so that I may enjoy the
fullness of life and glorify you among my fellows,
through Jesus Christ our Lord.

ANON

You know, Father, how often we sin with our tongues.
Keep me free from all untrue and unkind words;
consecrate my speech to your service and keep me
often silent, that my heart may speak to you
and listen for your voice, through Jesus Christ our Lord.

ANON

May it become the great employment of my time on earth,
Lord, to root out all the accursed habits of sin in me,
that in holiness of life, in humility and love, in chastity and
pure living, I may by your grace patiently wait for the coming
of our Lord Jesus.

JEREMY TAYLOR

Grant, Lord, that we may
live in your fear,
die in your favour,
rest in your peace,
rise in your power
and reign in your glory,
for the sake of your Son Jesus Christ our Lord.

WILLIAM LAUD

Turfmoss (*Sphagnum sp.*) with wood sorrel (*Oxalis acetosella*)

Private prayers

The Bible and the ancient service books of the church have long been a source of prayers. Bishop Lancelot Andrewes made up his own personal prayerbook from them and not long after his death in 1626 it was published for the first time. Editions and selections have gone on being printed ever since. Not everything in this section is his but the sources are the same. The Bible is the best prayerbook there is. If you find these prayers helpful look out for a copy—probably secondhand—of Andrewes' prayers. The Latin title under which they were often sold is Preces Privatae, *which explains the heading of this section!*

Praised are you Lord,
you alone do marvellous things.
Your glory fills all the earth for ever and ever.

Who can be compared with you, Lord?
Who is your like, majestic in holiness?
Saviour of the wretched from those too strong
    for them;
from those who prey on them.
Many times have you come to my rescue,
although I was rebellious still and disobedient,
you heard my cry,
looked with pity on my distress.

I will not forget your goodness to me.
    You forgive my sin,
    heal my suffering,
    carry my troubles,
    and surround me with constant love.
    You are my God, you save me.
In your hand lies escape from death.
My tongue shall cry out your glory,
and all creatures bless your name.

My whole being praises you.
Young men and girls,
old people and children too,
rich and poor alike
will come and adore you Lord,
bow down and honour your name.

God my King
I will extol your greatness,
praising you day after day,
your name for ever and ever.

Today I adore you,
and for as long as I live I will praise you.
May my thoughts please you.

You are my God, I thank you.
I will proclaim your greatness,
I will exalt you with all my heart
in company with all who serve you.

From the rising of the sun to its setting
your name, Lord, endures for ever
your renown throughout all generations.

Who can tell all the great things you have done?
Can I count them?
They outnumber the grains of the sand![1]

To God the eternal king,
the only God and ruler,
alone immortal;
living in light that no-one can approach.
None has ever seen you,
No-one can ever see you,
King of Kings, Lord of Lords,
To you be honour and dominion for ever and ever.[2]

Holy, holy, holy, Lord God almighty,
who was, and is, and is to come,
Heaven and earth, angels and humankind,
the air, the sea, give glory and honour and thanks
to him who sits on the throne,
who lives for ever and ever.
All the blessed spirits and souls of the righteous
cast their crowns before the throne
and worship him who lives for ever and ever.
You are worthy Lord to receive
glory, and honour and power
for you have created all things and for your pleasure they are
    and were created.

1 Lancelot Andrewes
2 1 Timothy

Great and marvellous are your works
Lord God almighty.
Just and true are your ways, King of Saints,
Your wisdom is infinite; your mercies are glorious
and I am not worthy Lord to appear in your presence,
before whom the angels hide their faces.
Holy and eternal Jesus, Lamb of God,
slain from the beginning of the world,
You have redeemed us by your blood out of every nation
and made us sovereigns and priests to our God:
We shall reign with you for ever.
Blessing, honour, glory and power
be to him who sits on the throne and to the Lamb
for ever and ever.[1]

Two things I recognise in myself, Lord:
   I am made in your image;
   I have defaced that likeness.
I admit to my fault.
But remember Lord,
by myself I can't do much about it.
Take from me what I have spoiled
leave in me what you have made.
Don't allow my stupidity and wickedness
to destroy what your goodness has redeemed.
Acknowledge in me what is yours;
take from me the sin that is mine.
   I come to you, the Almighty.
   I come to you, the Physician.
   Where I am blind, show me the way.
   Where I am sick in mind, heal me.
   Where I am in the stranglehold of habit, release me.[2]

1 Lancelot Andrewes, adapted by Jeremy Taylor
2 Lancelot Andrewes

To him who is able to keep me from falling,
and bring me faultless and joyful before his presence
to the only God our Saviour,
through Jesus Christ our Lord
be glory, majesty, might and authority,
from all ages, past, now, and forever and ever.[1]

God, I love you,
above everything else,
and for no other reason
except you, yourself.
   I want you;
   I long for you;
   Always, in all things, with all my heart and being,
   I look for you.

If you don't give me yourself when I come to die,
you will have given me nothing.
I am only looking for you because I hope to find you.

   This hope is like honey,
   it sweetens anything that happens.
   If you are not going to give me yourself,
   destroy this hope in me, for ever.
   Otherwise I shall pine away with love,
   for I shall always be empty.

But this is not your way with us,
most gracious, best and loving God.
Make me in this life
   always to love you for yourself before all things,
   to seek you in all things;
   And at the last in the life to come,
   to find and to keep you for ever.[2]

1 Jude
2 Lancelot Andrewes

Hart's tongue fern (*Phyllitis scolopendrium*)
with herb Robert (*Geranium robertianum*)

My God and King

Next to the Bible, a great source of ready-made prayers is to be found in our hymn books. True, some hymns are very bad, both in what they say about God, and how they say it. The ones that say it best, however, are usually written by men and women who not only love God but also love language too. They are poets. What a poet means is far more than the actual words used, so a poem is much the best way of expressing the greatest truths. But poems are not always easy to understand first time. Poets rarely begin and end a sentence in one line. Two of the poems here have deliberately been set out like a prayer, just to help you to make better sense of them. Please don't show them to English teachers, they'll only have apoplexy! To use a poem as a prayer say it very slowly to yourself—and remember a poem is meant to be read aloud. Then stop and think about what you've read. After a few minutes repeat the reading followed by the thinking. Leave plenty of space and silence to enable the good Lord to use the poet's words to get through to you.

Even such is Time, which takes in trust
Our youth, our joys, and all we have,
And pays us but with age and dust:
Who in the dark and silent grave,
When we have wandered all our ways,
Shuts up the story of our days:
And from which earth, and grave, and dust,
The Lord shall raise me up I trust.

WALTER RALEIGH

My spirit longs for thee
Within my troubled breast,
Though I unworthy be
Of so divine a guest.

Of so divine a guest,
Unworthy though I be,
Yet has my heart no rest
Unless it come from thee.

JOHN BYROM

There is a language writt'n on earth and sky
by God's own pen in silent majesty;
There is a voice that's heard and felt and seen
In spring's young shades and summer's endless green;
There is a book of poesy and spells
In which that voice in sunny splendour dwells;
There is a page in which that voice aloud
Speaks music to the few and not the crowd:
Though no romantic scenes my feet have trod,
The voice of nature as the voice of God
Appeals to me in every tree and flower,
Breathing his glory, magnitude and power.

JOHN CLARE

Batter my heart, three-personed God;
for, you as yet, but knock,
breath,
shine,
and seek to mend.

That I may rise, and stand,
o'erthrow me;
and bend your force,
to break, blow, burn,
and make me new.

I, like an usurped town (to another due),
labour to admit you, but oh to no end!
Reason, your viceroy in me,
me should defend,
But is captived,
and proves weak,
or untrue.

Yet dearly I love you,
and would be loved fain,
but am betrothed unto your enemy.
Divorce me,
untie, or break that knot again.
Take me to you.
Imprison me.
For I,
except you enthral me,
never shall be free;
Nor ever chaste,
Unless You ravish me.

JOHN DONNE

Away, vain world, bewitcher of my heart!
My sorrow show, my sins make me to smart!
   Yet will I not despair,
   But to my God repair—
   He has mercy aye,
   Therefore will I pray:
He has mercy aye, and loves me;
Though by his humbling hand he proves me.

What shall I say? Are all my pleasures past?
Shall worldly lusts now take their leave at last?
   Yea, Christ, these earthly toys
   Shall turn to heavenly joys,
   Let the world begone,
   I'll love Christ alone!
Let the world be gone—I care not.
Christ is my love alone—I fear not.

ALEXANDER MONTGOMERIE

O Most Mighty! O MOST HOLY!
   Far beyond the seraph's thought,
Art thou then so mean and lowly
   As unheeded prophets taught?

O the magnitude of meekness!
   Worth from worth immortal sprung;
O the strength of infant weakness,
   If eternal is so young!

If so young and thus eternal,
   Michael tune the shepherd's reed,
Where the scenes are ever vernal,
   And the loves be love indeed!

Nature's decorations glisten
   Far above their usual trim;
Birds on box and laurel listen,
   As so near the cherubs' hymn.[1]

Spinks[2] and ouzles[3] sing sublimely,
  'We too have a Saviour born,'
Whiter blossoms bursts untimely
  On the blest Mosaic thorn.[4]

God all-bounteous, all creative,
  Whom no ills from good dissuade,
Is incarnate, and a native
  Of the very world he made.

       CHRISTOPHER SMART

Love bade me welcome;
Yet my soul drew back,
Guilty of dust and sin.

But quick-eyed Love,
Observing me grow slack from my first entrance in,
Drew nearer to me,
Sweetly questioning if I lacked anything?

'A guest', I answered, 'worthy to be here.'
Love said, 'You shall be he.'
'I, the unkind, ungrateful? Ah my dear,
I cannot look on thee.'

Love took my hand,
and smiling, did reply,
'Who made the eyes, but I?'

'Truth, Lord,
but I have marred them;
Let my shame go where it doth deserve.'
'And know you not,' says Love,
'who bore the blame?'

1. The angels who appeared to the shepherds.
2. Chaffinches.
3. Blackbirds.
4. Glastonbury thorn, which flowers at Christmastide.

'My dear then I will serve . . .'
'You must sit down,' says Love,
'and taste my meat.'

So I did sit and eat.

GEORGE HERBERT

In thy word, Lord, is my trust,
To thy mercies fast I fly;
Though I am but clay and dust,
Yet thy grace can lift me high.

THOMAS CAMPION

Glory be to God for dappled things—
    For skies of couple-colour as a brinded cow;
        For rose-moles all in stipple upon trout that swim;
Fresh-firecoal chestnut-falls; finches' wings;
    Landscape plotted and pieced—fold, fallow, and plough;
        And all trades, their gear and tackle and trim.

All things counter, original, spare, strange:
    Whatever is fickle, freckled (who knows how?)
        With swift, slow; sweet, sour; adazzle, dim:
He fathers-forth whose beauty is past change:

Praise him.

GERARD MANLEY HOPKINS

O Thou who camest from above,
    The pure, celestial fire t'impart,
Kindle a flame of sacred love
    On the mean altar of my heart;
There let it for thy glory burn
    With inextinguishable blaze,
And trembling to its Source return,
    In humble prayer, and fervent praise.

Jesus confirm my heart's desire
    To work, and speak, and think for Thee;
Still let me guard the holy fire,
    And still stir up Thy gift in me:
Ready for all thy perfect will,
    My acts of faith and love repeat,
Till death Thy endless mercies seal,
    And make my sacrifice complete.

CHARLES WESLEY

Let all the world in every corner sing
          My God and King.
  The heavens are not too high,
  His praise may thither fly.
  The earth is not too low.
  His praises there may grow.
Let all the world in every corner sing.
          My God and King.
  The Church with psalms must shout,
  No door can keep them out.
  But above all the heart
  Must bear the longest part.
Let all the world in every corner sing
          My God and King.

GEORGE HERBERT

Marsh marigold (*Caltha palustris*)

String prayers

Some people find it difficult to keep utterly still and quiet. As soon as they settle down to pray, their nose itches and has to be scratched or a bruise they had almost forgotten starts to hurt. Is that you? If praying seems far too passive try it this way. Find a piece of cord 3 or 4 mm thick and about 40 cm long; picture cord or cushion edging is ideal, but thick string will do. Tie a large knot at either end, and in between equally spaced, ten smaller knots. Choose one of the prayers in this section and decide how long you are going to pray using this way of prayer—perhaps five minutes? Hold on to one of the large knots with your fingers and as you feel it say the Lord's Prayer. Now move on to the first small knot, say your chosen prayer and repeat it ten times, moving down your cord as you pray. Finally on the large knot at the end say the 'Glory to the Father' (top of page 2). Repeat the exercise again and again for the time allotted. While all this is going on you can also be thinking about God, or our Saviour, or perhaps praying for someone in need. The string keeps your hands busy: the prayers keep your mind and perhaps your tongue busy, and that leaves your heart for the Holy Spirit to keep busy.

Give me courage to trample on temptation and strength to break the chains of sin.

CHRISTINA ROSSETTI

Give me, O God of my prayer, the grace to continue waiting for you in prayer.

KARL RAHNER

God, of your goodness give me yourself for only in you have I all.

JULIAN OF NORWICH

Grant that we to whom you have given reason and speech may bless you with heart and lips.

CHRISTINA ROSSETTI

Help me to be in control of myself that I may become the servant of others. Help me to mature, not by doing often what I like, but what I should.

KARL RAHNER

Holy Spirit, cherish the little beginnings of goodness which you see flickering in me, and strengthen all my attempts to make them grow.

SIMON PATRICK

Holy Spirit, kindle the lamp of love in my life.

RABINDRANATH TAGORE

I am not my own, but the Lord's. He has bought me with a price and I have given myself to him again and again. Therefore I will glorify him with body and soul which are his.

SIMON PATRICK

It is glory enough to be your servant; it is grace enough that you are my Lord. Jesus, acknowledge what is yours in me and take from me all that is not yours.

ST BERNARDINE

Jesus, by the memory of your cross and passion, make me fear you; make me love you.

ST BRIDGET

Let me all my wits apply,
Thy great name to magnify
Whilst I live; and when I die.

GEORGE WITHER

Let me make my life simple, and straight as a recorder, for you to fill with music.

RABINDRANATH TAGORE

Let us be careful that no image but that of God takes shape in our souls.

ST COLUMBANUS

Lord, change my sins into penitence; my penitence into prayer and my prayer into thanksgiving.

JEREMY TAYLOR

Lord, cure our diseases, forgive our sins; lighten our burdens.

CHRISTOPHER SUTTON

Lord, instruct me in true poverty of spirit, in gentleness, in faith and in love of you and my neighbour.

JOHN WESLEY

Lord Jesus, I find you throned in my heart. It is enough. I know you are enthroned in heaven. My heart and heaven are one.

ANON

Lord, life is a constant battle. May I never grow weary in the fight, looking up to Jesus in whom we have the victory.

JOHN CALVIN

Lord, make me holy through your holiness, pure through your purity and loving through your love.

E. B. PUSEY

Lord, may I daily be more thirsty for both holiness and your glory.

JOHN WESLEY

Lord, may I love you for yourself and my neighbour for you.

JEREMY TAYLOR

Lord, may much of your love be in my heart and much of your presence in my work.

JOHN WESLEY

Lord, may your grace overpower my sin; may your strength uphold my weakness; may your peace dispel my sadness.

E. B. PUSEY

Lord, pity and pardon, direct and bless, sanctify and save all your children.

JEREMY TAYLOR

Make me remember, Lord, that every day is your gift and ought to be used according to your commands.

SAMUEL JOHNSON

Merciful Father, give me now your Holy Spirit that I may be strengthened for my work today.

ST JOHN OF KRONSTADT

O Saviour of men, save us from trusting in anything but you.

JOHN WESLEY

Sharpen my will, O God. May it be like a sword and cut all sinful thoughts out of my mind.

SCHENUTE OF ATRIPE

A SELECTION OF STRING PRAYERS FROM THE PSALMS

(Coverdale's translation in the *Book of Common Prayer*)

I will give thanks unto thee, O Lord, with my whole heart: I will speak of all thy marvellous works. (9.1)

I will sing of the Lord, because he hath dealt so lovingly with me: yea, I will praise the name of the Lord most Highest. (13.6)

In thy presence is the fulness of joy and at thy right hand there is pleasure for evermore. (16.12)

Unto thee, O Lord, will I lift up my soul: my God I have put my trust in thee. (25.1)

I believe verily to see the goodness of the Lord in the land of the living. (27.15)

God is the King of all the earth: sing ye praises with understanding. (47.7)

Make me a clean heart, O God: renew a right spirit within me. (51.10)

An offering of a free heart will I give Thee, and praise thy Name O Lord. (54.6)

My soul truly waiteth still upon God: for of him cometh my salvation. (62.1)

My soul thirsteth for thee, my flesh also longeth after thee. (63.2)

Thou O Lord God art the thing that I long for: thou art my hope. (71.4)

I will sing unto the Lord as long as I live: I will praise my God while I have my being. (104.33)

Thou art my God and I will thank Thee: Thou art my God and I will praise thee. (118.28)

Praise the Lord, O my soul; while I live will I praise the Lord: yea as long as I have any being, I will sing praises unto my God. (146.1)

ARROW PRAYERS

Some of the above prayers, and other short ones too, are very useful to be learnt by heart, to be prayed—shot up if you like—at odd moments, especially times of crisis or stress, throughout the day.

JESUS PRAYER

Another version of this way of prayer has been practised by Eastern Orthodox Christians in particular for many, many centuries. To help concentration they use a circular plaited knotted cord made of black goats' hair.

The form of prayer concentrates on the holy name of Jesus, which incidentally in Hebrew means 'Saviour'. We cannot be absolutely certain how our Lord's name would have been pronounced in Judea, but most scholars think it would have sounded something like 'Yeshua'. From that you can see immediately it is close to the name of an Old Testament hero, and the book of the Old Testament which bears his name, Joshua. They are indeed one and the same name.

The two forms of the prayer, much in use, come from the Scriptures too. They are:

Jesus Christ, Son of God, have mercy on me a sinner

Jesus Christ, Son of God, have mercy

To use it, concentrate on your breathing. Say the prayer aloud if you are alone, otherwise silently—as you breathe out. Remain silent as you inhale. It is a good idea to be kneeling upright—perhaps with the support of a prayer-stool. Repeat the prayer continuously. If you find your mind wandering, don't worry. Just renew your concentration on your prayer. Those who use the Jesus Prayer as the staple diet of their spiritual life set aside time each day—and use the prayer constantly. During the rest of the day, at those moments when the mind has nothing to concentrate on, they eventually fall back naturally into the rhythm of the prayer. The great saints who used the Jesus prayer used to take St Paul's instruction to the Thessalonian Christians to pray without ceasing quite literally!

YET ANOTHER WAY—'CHOPPING' PRAYER

Some Christians recognise the close connection between the 'affective way' of prayer (as the method of praying which has been described throughout this chapter is sometimes called) and the mantras used by those who practise Eastern religions. Mantra prayer consists of a rhythmic repetition of a single word. The last line of T. S. Eliot's poem The Waste Land *is a mantra, 'Shantih, shantih, shantih'. It means 'peace', and comes from an Indian holy book.*

One Christian approach to this kind of prayer is best described by a practical example.

Take the tenth verse of Psalm 46:

Be still and know that I am God.

Settle yourself for prayer so that you are both alert yet comfortable. Perhaps a few deep breaths and then say the verse slowly to yourself, aloud if you can. Repeat it a few times and then knock off the first three words. Your prayer will now be, Know that I am God. *Repeat that for a while and then chop off the last word.* Know that I am. *Repeat the shortened prayer for a bit and finally remove the words 'Know that'.*

Your prayer has now become just two words I am. *(Read Exodus chapter 3 verse 14 and you'll discover that 'I am' is one of the names of God.) Go on repeating the two words in prayer. You might find that after a little while, you will be adding to them one of the phrases that Jesus uses of himself in St John's gospel: e.g.* I am the resurrection and the life *or* I am the bread of life.

Before you begin to pray in this way don't forget to decide beforehand how much time you are going to give God, and stick to it. Should your mind wander, don't worry. As soon as you realise you are thinking about something or someone else, stop doing so, bring your mind back to your mantra and start again.

Pussy willow (*Salix caprea*)

Were you there?

The Olympic Games. Three flags are slowly fluttering to the top of their poles. Bands are playing, and you, standing proudly to attention on the podium, have a gold medal gleaming round your neck. Have your daydreams included that one?

Everyone has powers of imagination. Parents use them to anticipate the kinds of problems or even dangers that their children might meet. Those of us who worry a lot use ours as we face unknown possibilities—and get ourselves into quite a lather. Our imaginations are powerful agents in our human nature. And human nature is part of God's creation.

We can use our imaginations in our prayers, imagining ourselves present for example when Jairus came to Jesus to seek help for his daughter. The following pages have been designed to help you use stories from the Bible for imaginative prayer.

Jairus' daughter (Mark 5.22–23 and 35–43, TEV)

Jairus, an official of the local synagogue, arrived, and when he saw Jesus, he threw himself down at his feet and begged him earnestly, 'My daughter is very ill. Please come and place your hands on her, so that she will get well and live.'

Some messengers came from Jairus' house and told him, 'Your daughter has died. Why bother the Teacher any longer?'

Jesus paid no attention to what they said, but told him, 'Don't be afraid, only believe.' Then he did not let anyone else go on with him except Peter and James and his brother John. They arrived at Jairus' house, where Jesus saw the confusion and heard all the loud crying and wailing. He went in and said to them 'Why all this confusion? Why are you crying? The child is not dead—she is only sleeping.'

They laughed at him, so he put them all out, took the child's father and mother and his three disciples, and went into the room where the child was lying. He took her by the hand and said to her, 'Talitha, koum,' which means 'Little girl, I tell you to get up!'

She got up at once and started walking around. (She was twelve years old.) When this happened, they were completely amazed. But Jesus gave them strict orders not to tell anyone, and he said, 'Give her something to eat.'

WHAT TO DO

1. *To begin with you must choose a story from the Bible. Here I have taken the story of Jairus' little girl; there are four more examples on the following pages. Read the story through carefully, trying to remember the gist of the conversations reported in the text. That will probably mean you'll have to read it more than once. The questions beneath the passages of the other four examples are to help you explore the events in greater detail.*

2. *Settle into an upright chair, comfortable but not too comfortable: you want to keep alert. Sit up straight, close*

your eyes and slowly take ten deep breaths. You could have your hands on your knees or in your lap.

3. Now recall the story, imagining yourself as one of the characters. It could be Jairus himself, or his wife, the girl's mother, one of the twelve, one of the crowd, or one of those mourning the child. Don't hurry; try to see what Jesus is wearing. What is the look on his face? What does it feel like to be with him in this situation?

4. Respond to the events. If you chose to be the mother of the little girl, or Jairus himself, when she opens her eyes you would obviously be full of thanksgiving, delight and wonder. Let them spill over in your heart. In your thoughts move quite gently from the parents' praise to your own wonder and thanksgiving for the love of God as revealed in Jesus. For a brief while consider what difference the love of God makes to you and the way you live. Or what difference it might make? Resolve how it will, and offer your resolution to God, knowing that he is always ready to give you the power to make it possible.

5. Some people prefer to work this kind of prayer with these three ideas.

(i) First, go over the story in your imagination, watching Jesus all the time. In this method don't imagine yourself to be one of the characters in the gospel account; just be there yourself, eavesdropping, as it were!

JESUS IN YOUR EYES

(ii) Next look at your own life and try to pick out something from the story that could apply to it. For instance, the wonderful faith of Jairus who was convinced that Jesus could help him. 'Is my faith like that?'

JESUS IN YOUR MIND

(iii) Finally ask the Holy Spirit to awaken in yourself, whatever it is you have considered in the second section, and open your inner being to receive the grace of God.

JESUS IN YOUR HEART

Don't forget to finish your time of prayer with an act of thanksgiving to God our Father for revealing himself to us in his Son.

Story of Zacchaeus (Luke 19.1–10, JB)

When you read this story remember that tax collectors, sometimes called publicans, were considered to be both cheats and traitors, collecting cash for the Roman army of occupation.

Jesus entered Jericho and was going through the town when a man whose name was Zacchaeus made his appearance; he was one of the senior tax collectors and a wealthy man. He was anxious to see what kind of man Jesus was, but he was too short and could not see him for the crowd; so he ran ahead and climbed a sycamore tree to catch a glimpse of Jesus who was to pass that way. When Jesus reached the spot he looked up and spoke to him: 'Zacchaeus, come down. Hurry, because I must stay at your house today.' And he hurried down and welcomed him joyfully. They all complained when they saw what was happening. 'He has gone to stay at a sinner's house,' they said. But Zacchaeus stood his ground and said to the Lord, 'Look, sir, I am going to give half my property to the poor, and if I have cheated anybody I will pay him back four times the amount.' And Jesus said to him, 'Today salvation has come to this house, because this man too is a son of Abraham, for the Son of Man has come to seek out and save what was lost.'

How did the 'respectable' people feel about Zacchaeus? Would they easily believe his change of heart? Who are the people in your neck of the woods whom everybody dislikes or distrusts? How do you treat them?

Do you love me? (John 21.15–17, RSV)

When they had finished breakfast, Jesus said to Simon Peter, 'Simon, son of John, do you love me more than these?' He said to him, 'Yes, Lord; you know that I love you.' He said to him, 'Feed my lambs.' A second time he said to him, 'Simon, son of John, do you love me?' He said to him, 'Yes, Lord; you know that I love you.' Jesus said to him, 'Tend my sheep.' He said to him the third time, 'Simon, son of John, do you love me?' Peter was grieved because he said to him the third time, 'Do you love me?' And he said to him, 'Lord, you know everything; you know that I love you.' Jesus said to him, 'Feed my sheep.'

Why did Jesus ask Peter that question three times? Why was Peter upset? How do you feel when you've let someone down? When you've been let down?

Stuck up (Mark 9.33–37, NEB)

So they came to Capernaum; and when Jesus was indoors, he asked them, 'What were you arguing about on the way?' They were silent, because on the way they had been discussing who was the greatest. He sat down, called the Twelve, and said to them, 'If anyone wants to be first, he must make himself last of all and servant of all.' Then he took a child, set him in front of them, and put his arm round him. 'Whoever receives one of these children in my name,' he said, 'receives me; and whoever receives me, receives not me but the One who sent me.'

Why are people so worried about their position in the world? What good does it do? Why do you find it difficult when others push in front of you? How do you react?

Total loyalty (Ruth 1.14–17, RSV)

The Old Testament can be used in the same way as the New. Imagine yourself into the scene. As well as responding to what happens look at one of the characters as if he—in this case as if she, Ruth—were Christ: or at least regard her words as his.

Then they lifted up their voices and wept again; and Orpah kissed her mother-in-law, but Ruth clung to her. And Naomi said, 'See your sister-in-law has gone back to her people and

to her gods; return after your sister-in-law.' But Ruth said,
'Entreat me not to leave you or to return from following you;
for where you go I will go, and where you lodge I will lodge;
your people shall be my people, and your God my God;
where you die I will die, and there will I be buried. May the
Lord do so to me and more also if even death parts me from
you.'

*As well as hearing Christ use Ruth's words to you, you can also
use her words to Naomi as a prayer dedicating yourself to God.
Many parts of the Old Testament can be employed in this way.*

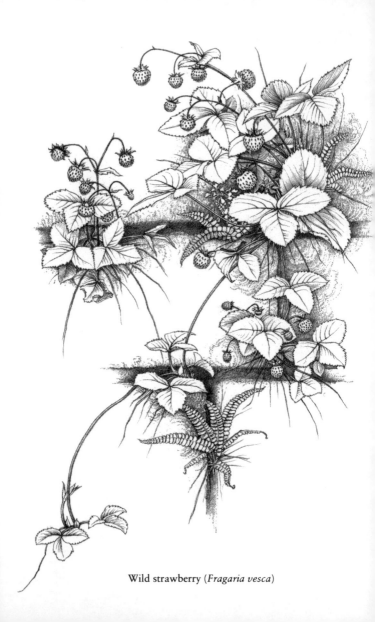

Wild strawberry (*Fragaria vesca*)

Our Father

The prayer which Jesus gave his disciples is a model. Most Christians know it off by heart but in the early days of the Church it was not taught to them until they had been baptised. Simone Weil, the French Jewess who managed to join the Free French in exile in England during the Second World War, became a believer but was never baptised. She used it every day, carefully considering each word. Whenever her mind wandered from the prayer she'd go right back to the beginning and start again. It sometimes took her an hour or more to complete it. Try it yourself but don't get too intense—it could be dangerous. Or you might find it easier to concentrate on each petition, pondering, for instance, what we mean when we pray 'Our Father' rather than 'My Father' and so on. The five prayers in this section come from our own and the previous three centuries. They are expansions or paraphrases of the Lord's Prayer. Never use all five at one pray-in! You'll find another in the collection of litanies on pages 122ff.

Father of all
you are the holy one.
    Your name is above every name
    to be hallowed and worshipped by all.
    Frequently I ignore you,
    and I don't always reverence your name.
    I'm sorry.
    I want my life, my words and my thoughts
    to bring glory to you and your name.
I want your kingdom
to be established
    —in me.
    Give me your help.
    —on earth.
    Let me help to bring it.
Let the old me, my sinful nature, die and your life rise in me,
that your will not mine may be done.
    Give us what we need for
    —the well being of our bodies
    —the peace of the world
    —our journey to you.

Forgive me my wrongdoing
    —my shameful deeds,
    —my frequent lapses into sin,
    —my daily wallowings in evil.
Help me to become aware of those things in me
that I don't realise prevent me from doing your will.
    Neither let me enter nor be led into temptation;
    remember I am small of spirit and very weak.
Deliver me from evils past, present and to come
    —in myself
    —in others
    —of disease.
Deliver and save me Lord. Amen.

LANCELOT ANDREWES

Most merciful Father in heaven, who sees everything that is done on earth, may your name be hallowed by all your creatures, O great and holy God. May your kingdom come, set up in this world by the preaching of your gospel. May all nations submit themselves to you and to your son, Jesus Christ. Let your son reign in the hearts of men and women and your will be done among us as it is among the angels in heaven. Give me today my daily bread, and every day of my life give me what is necessary to maintain my health and strength, that I may be more capable of serving you. For the sake of the death and passion of your dear son, forgive me my sins, and enable me from my heart to forgive those who have sinned against me. Lead me not into temptation, nor let me run carelessly into danger of sinning but deliver me from the evil one, and from all his tricks to defile and destroy me. The kingdom and the government of all things belong to you. You have power to do what I ask, and all honour and glory are yours for ever and ever. Amen.

ISAAC WATTS

Our Father in heaven, in whom we live and move and have our being, grant that all Christians may live worthily as your children, doing what is good because we are yours. You have made us yours by adoption; may we choose to be yours as well.

Your name is great, wonderful and holy. May we glorify you not only with our lips but in our lives, that all may see good in us and so glorify you our Father in heaven.

May all the countries of the world become the Kingdom of our Lord and his Christ, and may all who own you as King become your faithful and obedient subjects.

We adore your goodness in making your will known to us in your holy word. May your word rule our wills, our desires, our actions. May we sacrifice our wills to your will, accepting your choices for us and others and adoring your providence in the government of the world.

Father, you know our needs, supply them all with your blessing, but above all give us the Bread which nourishes to eternal life, and grace to share our food with those who have none.

Forgive us our sins. Make us conscious of your goodness, love and patience towards us, and grant that we may from our hearts forgive our brothers and sisters who sin against us.

Support us under all our trials and grant that we may live peacefully with a good conscience. From all sin and wickedness and from everlasting death, from our human nature which always lurches towards evil, from the temptations of the world and from falling again into sins which we have once repented, deliver us, good Lord.

By your almighty power, O King of heaven, for the glory of your name and for the love of the Father, grant us all blessings for which you have taught us to pray. To him that is able to do even more than we can ask or think, to him be glory in the Church by Christ Jesus to the ages of ages. Amen.

THOMAS WILSON

Enable me, O Father, to pray with all my heart as your Son Jesus has taught me, that your name may be hallowed and your kingdom come. Give me earnest zeal for your honour. May I never forget you; never drive you from my thoughts; never imagine that I do anything without you. Rule within me. Give us through the Holy Spirit your kingdom of righteousness, peace and joy. Let your holy will be done with us, and in us and by us all, even as it is done in heaven where saints and angels serve you without weariness, beholding your glory and listening night and day to your voice.

Father, we ask you to provide us our food. Day by day, in body and mind, in soul and spirit, give each one of us what you see will be for our good. Give us what you know would be right of health and strength, of comfort and pleasure, of wisdom, discretion and skills, of energy and success in this life; and your blessing Lord, with them. In whatever happens to us may we fear no evil. Give us evermore that bread of life which is Christ Jesus and that water of life which is the Holy Spirit.

Father, forgive me my sins as I forgive those who sin against me, for the sake of our Lord Jesus Christ who bore our sins and washed away our guilt. Pardon us, Father, with your free forgiveness and fill us with that spirit of forgiveness which means peace with everyone.

Suffer us not, Father, to be tempted above our strength, but with every temptation provide also a way for us to escape, giving us grace to use it. Keep us from evil, from all sins and wickedness; from carelessness and taking you for granted; from coldness, hardness and even contempt for your word; from an ungodly life and from eternal death. Lord evermore deliver us. You are our Father, and we your children. Keep us always yours and grant us daily to increase more and more in our response to your Holy Spirit until we come to your everlasting kingdom, Through Jesus Christ our Lord. Amen.

C. J. VAUGHAN

Heavenly Father, we are yours,
created by your word and your spirit:
Chosen, as you chose the Israelites, to be your people.
You have spoken to us in your Son, who is your word.
In his flesh you made yourself real to us,
so we can understand what you are saying.
We do not live in a world without you.
We have heard your voice through your Church and its
    work.
Baptised, we have our being in that Church.

Father, in your Son you have reconciled the world to
    yourself,
abolishing sin and all its consequences.
May we cease to misunderstand or oppose your purposes;
May we stop contradicting or misrepresenting the gospel;
May our mingling of light and darkness not last for ever.
In your Son your kingdom has appeared.
Your will has been done,
and will be done,

just as it is unceasingly in heaven,
working itself out in the course of time.
Father, deliver us from our disobedience;
Set us free from all our contradictions.

Give us what we need, our daily food.
When we receive it we know that we shall live with you;
Everything you give us brings the promise
of that living bread from heaven.
We know you have prepared a banquet for us;
and we hear the invitation to be your guests.

Father, you have forgiven our sins.
In the person of your Son, you the holy and righteous God,
have changed places with us, the unrighteous.
In Jesus Christ you, O God, became the new man who will
    never die.
You have created a sinless new race round the cross of your
    Son:
You have given us the Holy Spirit so that he may live in us.
May I put on that new creation, ceasing to live for myself.
Make me holy in spite of what I am, or have been.

Father, shield us from the possibility of evil
from which we could not protect ourselves.
Without you, our efforts to overcome temptation can only
    make matters worse;
For the kingdom, the power and the glory belong,
not to us,
not to Christian people,
not even to the very religious,
but to you.
You have loved us, and you love us still;
You are our king, the almighty in whom we put our trust,
who can and will give us all that is good. Amen.

> *Based on an interpretation given by* KARL BARTH, *in
> accordance with the thought of the Reformers*

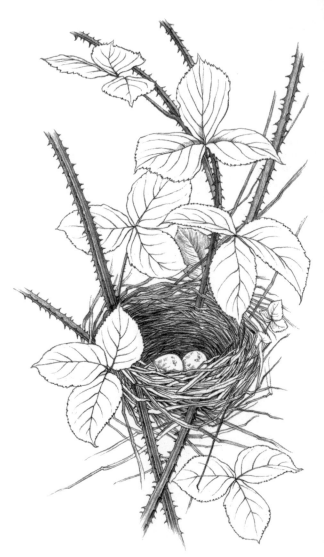

Blackcap nest (*Sylvia atricapilla*)

Prayers of saints—and sinners!

Many of these prayers will be unfamiliar to you, though you'll recognise some of their authors. Others you will know. You'll know immediately the prayer which begins 'Lord make me an instrument of your peace'. It appears as by St Francis of Assisi, but it is by no means certain that it is his. St Patrick's prayer, sometimes called 'St Patrick's Breastplate', is very long. Its actual title is 'The Deer Cry'. Don't be afraid to use only part of it, if that is what you want. The prayers are printed more or less in order of their composition. Why not add others that appeal to you—or your own?

God, you can do anything;
Take pity on me.
Make me not merely listen to what you tell us,
but do it as well.
Destroy in me what you know needs to be destroyed;
give life to what should live.
Grant that I may,
    believe in my heart,
    declare with my lips
    and prove by my deeds
that I am yours,
baptised into your Son Jesus Christ,
by the power of the Holy Spirit.

Adapted from two sermons by ORIGEN

Keep us, Lord, from useless arguments and grant us a
constant profession of the truth. Preserve us in the faith, true
and undefiled; so that we may ever hold fast that which we
professed when we were baptised into the Name of the
Father and of the Son and of the Holy Spirit, that we may
have you for our Father, may live in your Son in the
fellowship of the Holy Spirit, through the same your son,
Jesus Christ our Lord.

ST HILARY *of Poitiers*

O Thou, who art the light of the minds that know thee;
and the strength of the wills that serve thee;
Help us so to know thee that we may truly love thee,
so to love thee, that we may fully serve thee,
whom to serve is perfect freedom;
Through Jesus Christ our Lord.

ST AUGUSTINE *of Hippo*

Rich in grace and mercy, you are willing to purify all sinners
from their guilt. Have pity on me. You take sinfulness from
us, Lord Christ; when we repent you make us welcome. My
sins have thrown me down. I could not have been more
determined on my own ruin if I had rushed over a precipice.

Who but you, you who in the first place made me an image
of yourself, can restore me? It was my own free choice that
made me a slave of sin. Deliver me, Lord, in your mercy.

Adapted from a prayer attributed to BISHOP RABBULA

The Deer Cry

Today I go
Protected by the might of the Threefold God,
Believing in the Trinity,
Confessing the Unity
of the creator of all things.

Today I go
In the strength of Christ's birth and his baptism;
In the strength of Christ's cross and his burial;
In the strength of his Resurrection and Ascension;
In the strength of his coming as Judge.

Today I go
In the strength of the love of the Cherubim,
   the obedience of Angels,
   the service of Archangels,
   the hope of the Resurrection,
   the word of the prophets,
   the gospel of the apostles,
   the faith of confessors,
   the holy deeds of good men and women.

Today I go
through the power of the heavens,
   light of the sun,
   radiance of the moon,
   splendour of fire,
   speed of lightning,
   swiftness of wind,
   depths of the seas,
   stability of the earth,
   durability of rock.

Today I go
in the strength of God to pilot me,
in the might of God to uphold me,
by the wisdom of God to guide me,
through the eye of God to search out my way,
with the ear of God to hear me,
with the word of God to speak for me,
with the hand of God to guard me,
by the way of God to point me the road,
with the shield of God to protect me,
and the hosts of God to save me:
    from the snares of the devil,
    from temptation and vice,
    from everyone who wishes me ill,
    near and far,
    alone and in a crowd.

All these powers today are between me and all evil;
against every cruel and merciless power that may oppose me;
against lying prophets,
    black falsehoods,
    spurious teaching,
    witchcraft and idolatry,
    everything that can corrupt.

Christ shield me today,
    against all attacks of the enemy of human kind,
    against accident,
    against foolishness,
    against unsound judgement,
    against malice and violence.

Christ be with me,
Christ before me,
Christ above me.
Christ on my right hand, Christ on my left hand.
Christ when I lie down,
Christ when I sit down,
Christ when I stand.

Christ in the heart of everyone who thinks of me,
Christ in the mouth of everyone who speaks about me,
Christ in every eye that sees me,
Christ in every ear that hears me.

Today I go
Protected by the might of the Threefold God,
Believing in the Trinity,
Confessing the Unity
of the creator of all things.

ST PATRICK

Gracious and Holy Father,
give us wisdom to know you,
intelligence to understand you,
perseverance to search for you,
patience to wait for you,
eyes to see you,
a heart to meditate on you,
and a life to proclaim you,
through the power of the Spirit of Jesus Christ our Lord.

ST BENEDICT

O God, who for our redemption didst give thine only
begotten Son to the death of the cross, and by his glorious
resurrection hast delivered us from the power of the enemy.
Grant us to die daily to sin, that we may evermore live with
him in the joy of his resurrection; through the same Jesus
Christ our Lord.

ST GREGORY *and American Book of Common Prayer*,
1789

I pray you, good Jesus, that as you have given me the grace
to drink in with joy the word that gives knowledge of you, so
in your goodness you will grant me to come at length to
yourself, the source of all wisdom, to stand before your face
for ever.

VENERABLE BEDE

O eternal Light,
   shine into our hearts.
O eternal Goodness,
   deliver us from evil.
O eternal Power,
   be our strength.
O eternal Wisdom,
   dispel the darkness of our ignorance.
O eternal Pity,
   show mercy on us.
Grant that we may ever seek your countenance with all our
heart, mind, and strength. And in your infinite mercy enable
us to reach your holy presence.

ALCUIN

O Lord, you are my Lord and my God, yet I have never seen
   you.
You have created and redeemed me, and have conferred on
   me all my goods, yet I know you not.
I was created in order that I might know you, but I have not
   yet attained the goal of my creation.
I confess, O Lord, and give you thanks, that you have
   created me in your image, so that I might be mindful of
   you and contemplate you and love you.
I seek not to understand in order that I may believe; rather, I
   believe in order that I may understand. Amen.

ST ANSELM

Grant, Lord, that I may hold on to you without letting go;
worship you without growing tired; serve you without giving
up; faithfully seek you; happily find you, for ever possess
you, the one only God who is blessed for ever and ever.

ST ANSELM

Almighty, immortal, just and merciful God, give to us poor
creatures to do for you that which we know to be your will,
and to will always that which is well pleasing to you, so that
inwardly purified, illumined and enkindled by the flame of

68

the Holy Spirit we may be able to follow in the footprints of
our Lord Jesus Christ, and by your grace at length come to
you the Most High: who in perfect trinity and simple unity
live and reign God almighty, for ever and ever. Amen.

ST FRANCIS *of Assisi*

Canticle of Brother Sun

All-highest, all powerful, good Lord,
to you be praise, glory and honour
and every blessing.
To you alone they are due,
and no-one is worthy to speak your name.

Be praised, my Lord, in all your creatures,
especially Brother Sun,
who makes daytime.
Through him you give us light.
He is beautiful, radiant with great splendour,
and he is a sign
that tells, All-Highest, of you.

Be praised, my Lord, for Sister Moon and the stars:
you formed them in the sky,
bright, precious and beautiful.

Be praised, my Lord, for Brother Wind:
for the air and the clouds;
for fair, and every kind of weather,
by which you give your creatures food.

Be praised, my Lord, for Sister Water,
who is most useful and humble,
lovely and chaste.

Be praised, my Lord, for Brother Fire,
through whom you light up the night for us:
he is beautiful and jolly,
lusty and strong.

Be praised, My Lord, for our sister Mother Earth,
who keeps us, and feeds us,
bringing forth fruits of many kinds,
with coloured flowers and plants as well.

Be praised, my Lord, for those who forgive
for love of you,
or cope with sickness and vexation.
Blessed are those who bear these things peaceably
because, All-Highest,
they will be granted a crown by you.

Be praised, my Lord, for our Sister, Bodily Death,
whom no-one can escape.
Woe to those who die in mortal sin!
Blessed are those whom she will find
doing your holy will,
for to them the second death
will do no harm.

Bless and praise my Lord,
thank him, and serve him
in all humility.

St Francis *of Assisi*

Lord, make me an instrument of your peace.
   Where there is hatred, let me sow love;
   Where there is injury, pardon;
   Where there is doubt, faith;
   Where there is despair, hope;
   Where there is darkness, light;
   Where there is sadness, joy.

O Divine Master, grant that I may not so much seek
  to be consoled, as to console;
  to be understood, as to understand;
  to be loved, as to love.
For it is in giving that we receive,
it is in pardoning that we are pardoned,
it is in dying that we are born to eternal life.

Ascribed to ST FRANCIS *of Assisi*

O Lord, into your hands, and into the hands of your holy
angels, I commit and entrust this day, myself, my relatives,
my friends, my enemies, and all Christian people.

  By the intercession of the Blessed Virgin Mary, and of all
your saints, keep us from all evil and unruly desires, from all
sins and temptations, from sudden death, and from the pains
of hell. Enlighten my heart with the grace of your Holy
Spirit.

  Grant that I may ever be obedient to your commandments
and never let me be separated from you.

ST EDMUND RICH *of Abingdon*

Thanks be to thee my Lord Jesus Christ,
For all the benefits thou hast won for me,
For all the pains and insults thou hast borne for me,
O most merciful Redeemer, Friend and Brother;
May I know thee more clearly;
Love thee more dearly;
And follow thee more nearly;
For ever and ever.

ST RICHARD *of Chichester*

O Tender Father,
You gave me more,
much more than I ever thought to ask for.
I realise our human desires
can never really match what you long to give us.
Thanks, and again thanks, O Father,
for giving me what I prayed for,
and also for giving what
I never realised I needed.

ST CATHERINE *of Siena*

Christ my King,
I want you and you alone
as my Lord and Lord of everyone.
You have redeemed us, given yourself as ransom for my sin,
and the sin of all the world.
You have delivered us from the power of evil.

Gather us all into one flock.
Do not allow us to remain divided and in conflict with one
another.
If you draw the one, do not reject the other, since for all of us
you were delivered, and all have been cleansed by your precious
blood.
If you help me, help others as well.
Grant to each of us the same longing for you.
May we be brought together by you our common goal.
May divisions never rise to separate us, for then one of us is
separated from you.

JOHN BESSARION

Lord Jesus Christ, the way, the truth and the life, suffer me
not to stray from you, the way, nor to distrust you, the truth,
nor to rest in anything else but you, the life. Teach me by the
Holy Spirit what to believe, what to do, and where to relax
and rest. For your own name's sake, I ask it.

DESIDERIUS ERASMUS

God of all peoples, be mindful of those without belief.
Created in your image,
they do not know you, or your Son Jesus Christ, their
    Saviour,
who died for them.
By the prayers and labours of your Church,
free them from ignorance and unbelief,
and lead them to worship you.

ST FRANCIS XAVIER

Almighty God, your Holy Spirit
fills the whole world, living with us and within us.
Grant that I may not profane his sanctuary by my sins,
but strive to consecrate myself to your service, that your
    Name
through Jesus may be glorified for ever.

JOHN CALVIN

O Lord, give me a good digestion as well as
something to digest.
Give me health of body, as well as
the sense to keep it healthy.
Give me a holy soul, O Lord, which keeps
its eyes on beauty and purity, so that
it will not be afraid on seeing sin.
Give me a soul that knows nothing of
boredom, groans, and sighs.
Never let me be overly concerned
for this inconstant thing I call me.
Lord, give me a sense of humour, so that I
may take some happiness from this life,
and share it with others.

ST THOMAS MORE

Give me, Lord, a humble, quiet, peaceable,
patient, tender and loving mind, and to all my thoughts,
words and deeds a taste of your Holy Spirit.
Give me a living faith, a firm hope,
fervent love of my fellows and you.
Take from me all lukewarmness in prayer,
and make me delight in thinking of you and your grace
and love towards me and everyone.
The things that I pray for give me grace to work at,
through Jesus Christ our Lord.

ST THOMAS MORE

Lord God, may I be troubled by nothing,
Frightened by nothing.
Everything changes,
but you don't change.
Patience obtains everything.
I shall want nothing if
I possess you.
You alone, God, are all that I need.

ST TERESA *of Avila*

Dearest Lord, teach me to be generous,
to serve thee as thou deservest,
to give, and not to count the cost,
to fight, and not to heed the wounds,
to toil and not to seek for rest,
to labour and not to ask for any reward
save that of knowing that we do thy will;
Through Jesus Christ our Lord.

ST IGNATIUS LOYOLA

When you feel sleep to be coming pray:

Our Lord Jesus Christ my watchman and keeper,
take me to thy care; grant that while my body is sleeping my
mind may watch in thee, and be made joyful by some sight of
that celestial and heavenly life, wherein thou art the King and

Prince, together with the Father and the Holy Spirit; and thy angels and holy souls are most happy citizens. Oh! purify my soul, keep clean my body, that in both I may please thee sleeping and waking for ever.

JOHN BRADFORD

Let your mighty hand and outstretched arm, Lord God, be my
    defence:
your mercy and loving-kindness in your dear Son Jesus Christ,
my salvation; your all-time word, my instruction;
the grace of the life-giving Spirit,
my comfort and consolation to the end, and at the end.

Knox's Book of Common Order, 1569

Look, Lord, on an empty vessel that needs to be filled. In faith I am weak, strengthen me. In love I am cold, warm me and make me fervent that my love may go out to my neighbour. I doubt and am unable to trust you completely. Lord, strengthen my faith and trust in you. You are all the treasure I possess. I am poor, you are rich, and you came to have mercy on the poor. I am a sinner, you are goodness. From you I can receive goodness, but I can give you nothing. Therefore I shall stay with you.

MARTIN LUTHER

O Lord, when thou givest to thy servants to endeavour any
    great matter, grant us also to know that it is not the
    beginning, but the continuing of the same until it be
    thoroughly finished that yieldeth the true glory:
Through him who for the finishing of thy work laid down his
    life, our Redeemer, Jesus Christ.

FRANCIS DRAKE

O Lord God, thou art love,
and he that dwelleth in love dwelleth in thee,
and thou in him; grant that in this world we may so dwell
together through love, thou in us, by thy Holy Spirit, and we
in thee by faith, that after our departure from this vale of
misery we may be placed with thee in thy heavenly mansion
and so continue with thee in glory for ever and ever.

THOMAS BECON

Wilt thou forgive that sin where I begun,
   Which was my sin, though it were done before?
Wilt thou forgive that sin through which I run
   And do run still, though still I do deplore?
   When thou hast done,[1] thou hast not done:
   For I have more.

Wilt thou forgive that sin which I have won
   Others to sin, and made my sin their door?
Wilt thou forgive that sin which I did shun
   A year or two, but wallowed in a score?
   When thou hast done, thou hast not done:
   For I have more.

I have a sin of fear, that when I've spun
   My last thread, I shall perish on the shore;
But swear by thyself that at my death thy Son
   Shall shine as he shines now and heretofore;
   And having done that, thou hast done:
   I fear no more.

JOHN DONNE

1 If you remember that the author's name rhymes with 'done' you will
appreciate more the final lines of each stanza.

Most gracious Father fill your Church with all truth; in all
truth with all peace. Where it is corrupt, purge it; where it is
in error, direct it; where anything is wrong, reform it; where
it is right, strengthen and confirm it; where it is in great
want, supply its needs, where it is divided and torn apart;
heal and restore it for the sake of Jesus, Lord of the Church.

WILLIAM LAUD

My God and King, you only know what is truly best for me.
Only your love can give it me, only your power can make it
for me, and only in you can I enjoy it for ever. Give me grace
in this world to trust in your goodness, to seek, receive and
use your strength in your service to the end of my life,
through Jesus Christ our Lord.

GEORGE WITHER

Lord Jesus, lift from me the misery which love of self,
heedless of your glory, may draw from my sufferings, or
from my unfulfilled hopes and worldly ambitions. Make my
sorrow like your sorrow. From now onwards let me not
desire my health and strength except to use both in you, for
you and with you. You alone know what is good for me, for
you are Lord of all. Conform my will to yours, that I may
humbly obey you, confident in your love.

BLAISE PASCAL

Come, blessed spirit, into our hearts;
enlighten our understanding with your heavenly light;
warm our affections with your holy fire;
purge away all our dross;
burn up all our chaff;
renew our spirits;
separate our sin and evil from us;
unite us in your love;
subdue us to yourself;
teach our hearts to think,
our tongues to speak,
our hands to act,

our feet to move only to your will.
Settle yourself in us and dwell in us and
dwell with us to teach us with all our powers to praise
you here on earth. That we may one day praise you with the
Father and Son in heaven.

MARK FRANK

Lord, enlighten my understanding that I may know you:
sanctify my affections that I may love you and put the fear of
you in my heart that I may dread to offend you, through
Jesus Christ our Lord.

THOMAS KEN

Lord of love, keep me from passing judgement rashly on
others, that I may think and hope the best of all and love
everyone for the sake of Jesus Christ our loving Lord and
Saviour.

BENJAMIN JENKS

Whatever else you withhold from me, lover of mankind,
satisfy me with your likeness. Renew my heart in the whole
image of your Christ. Purge me from self-will, pride and
vanity. Fill me with faith and love, gentleness and
long-suffering. Let no guile be in my mouth, no injustice on
my hands. Draw me to you. Let me be emptied of myself and
then fill me with all peace and joy in believing, and let
nothing separate me from your love in time or in eternity,
through Jesus Christ our Lord.

JOHN WESLEY

My God, I don't begin to live as I know I should. I am attracted by things which are really pointless. I love anything better than giving time to you. I'm eager to get away from you. There are hardly any amusements I would not rather enjoy than set myself to think of you. Give me grace, Father, to be utterly ashamed of my own reluctance. Rouse me and make me desire you with my whole heart. Teach me to love you, for you are my eternal reward.

JOHN HENRY NEWMAN

Lord Jesus Christ, you know of what we are made, remake us, I pray, in your image, after your likeness, that having served you humbly here in your kingdom of grace, we may hereafter serve you triumphantly in the kingdom of glory, and being changed from glory to glory may see you face to face. Amen.

CHRISTINA ROSSETTI

Father, I abandon myself into your hands;
do with me what you will.
Whatever you may do, I thank you;
I am ready for all, I accept all;
let only your will be done in me,
and in all your creatures—
I wish no more than this, O Lord.
Into your hands I commend my soul
and offer it to you
with all the love of my heart;
for I love you, Lord,
and so need to give myself,
to surrender myself,
into your hands without reserve
and with boundless confidence,
for you are my Father.

CHARLES DE FOUCAULD

O Lord Jesus Christ, you prayed for your disciples that they might be one, as you are one with the Father. Draw us to yourself that in common love and obedience to you we may be united to one another in the fellowship of the one spirit, that the world may believe that you are Lord, to the glory of God the Father.

WILLIAM TEMPLE

Jesus,
if I follow you, I shall discover,
there is no way to peace that is secure.
Peace must be dared.
I cannot have my safety guaranteed,
for that would mean I distrusted
those with whom I want to be at peace.
By your Spirit,
help me in faith and obedience,
to give myself entirely to your law of love;
leaving the outcome in the Father's hands;
your Father and mine.

Based on some words of
DIETRICH BONHOEFFER

O Christ, so great is your attachment to every human being that wherever people are, even unknown to us, you are there, present.

For you, each one of us is sacred. We do not belong to ourselves, and no-one belongs to us.

We are yours, as you are God's.

When we are confined in our own prisons, your gift to us is to overcome barriers to discover a communion with you. When conflicts and divisions separate people, you call us to be tireless seekers after communion with everyone.

BROTHER ROGER *of Taizé*

How easy it is for me to live with you, Lord!
How easy it is for me to believe in you! When my thoughts
get stuck or my mind collapses, when the cleverest people
don't see further than this evening and do not know what
must be done tomorrow, you send down to me clear
confidence that you exist and that you will see to it that not
all the ways of goodness are blocked, for even I have been
able to shed abroad the radiance of your glory. And where I
am not able to do so, that means you have allotted this to
others.

ALEXANDER SOLZHENITSYN

Lord, whenever we follow you, guided by your Spirit, your
kingdom is brought a little nearer. Now we still live by faith
and in affliction beneath the shadow of your cross. But it is
in this way that your true kingdom comes, the realm of truth
and light, the kingdom of holiness and grace, of justice, love
and peace. Give us the grace to follow you and imitate you
faithfully.

KARL RAHNER

Field bindweed (*Convolvulus arvensis*)

Prayers of preparation

Sunday, the first day of the week as well as the second day of the weekend is the Christian holy day. It is the day of the Resurrection. Every Christian ought to try to share in worship on that day, particularly in the Eucharist. The prayer that follows could be used especially on those Sundays when you can't, don't, or won't make it to church.

All powerful Lord,
creator of all things,
for our sakes, your Word was born a human being,
and given the name of Jesus.
When he was baptised in the Jordan,
You claimed him as your Chosen One.
With your consent he suffered and died for us,
Yet through your might you raised him from the dead.
On Sunday, celebrating the Resurrection,
we rejoice because he conquers death,
and sheds abroad the light of everlasting life.
Fill me with your Spirit
to recognise all you have done,
that being aware of the greatness of your blessings,
my heart may overflow with your praises.

Adapted from a prayer in the Apostolic
Constitutions

FOR HOLY COMMUNION

Bishop Simon Patrick in his little Book for Beginners, *first published in 1662, wrote this:* The Holy Communion will be a means to make you observe his commandments 'with love and delight', which if they be wanting, your obedience will be little worth. For without 'love' all you do will not be acceptable to Christ; and unless you 'delight' in what you do, it will not be acceptable to yourself. *That's still true. Try to spend some time preparing for Holy Communion—on Saturday, before you go to sleep, or on Friday or Thursday if you've a hectic weekend ahead.*

Many of the prayers in this section have been adapted, from St Thomas Aquinas, Lancelot Andrewes, E. B. Pusey, or Bishop Patrick's little book.

As watchmen look for the morning, so do we look for you, O Christ. Come with the new day and make yourself known to us in the breaking of the bread, for you are our God for ever and ever.

Jesus hath spoke the Word,
His will my reason is,
Do this in memory of thy Lord,
Jesus hath said, Do this!

He bids me eat the Bread,
He bids me drink the Wine;
No other motive, Lord, I need
No other Word than Thine.

I cheerfully comply
With what my Lord doth say;
Let others ask a reason why,
My glory is to obey.

Because He saith, Do this,
This I will always do,
Till Jesus come in glorious bliss
I thus His death will shew.

CHARLES WESLEY

By the outward signs of bread and wine, you, my Saviour,
make it possible for me, sharing in your nature, to become
inseparably one with you: for we who eat the bread of
heaven, shall live the life of heaven.

Lord Jesus Christ, bread of life, nourish to life eternal those
who will receive the sacrament of your body and blood.
Purify our bodies, illuminate our spirits and satisfy our
hearts, that we may build our hopes on your sure and
gracious promise that loving you and abiding in your love,
we may have our hearts in heaven.

Lord, enter in and take possession of me. In your honour the
very stones would cry out; make my stony heart an
instrument of your praise. Let me cover your way with
flowers of goodness, and by your help, triumph over all my
difficulties and sins, laying my victories at your feet, and at
last follow you to the heavenly Jerusalem.

Good Jesus, of your tender love prepare a place in my heart
for yourself. Empty my being of every feeling, thought,
emotion, desire, purpose, anxiety, hope, fear which may
interfere with your love. Open me wholly to receive you. Let
nothing shut you out, nor let anything be closed to you.
Cleanse me by your Spirit that I may love you totally, being
entirely filled with you. Enlightened and warmed by you,
may you live in me for ever.

Send down your grace, O heavenly Father that we may all
receive the fullness of Christ from your hand. Empty us of
our sins; empty us of ourselves that we may be only filled
with you. Do not reject us as too unworthy. Fill us every day
with the fullness of your grace and leave us not to our own

weakness, that we may go on from grace to grace; from strength to strength; from virtue to virtue; till we come to be filled with the fullness of joy and pleasure and grace and glory for evermore.

Anima Christi

Soul of Christ sanctify me;
Body of Christ save me;
Blood of Christ inebriate[1] me;
Water from the side of Christ wash me;
Passion of Christ strengthen me;
O good Jesu hear me;
Within your wounds hide me;
Suffer me not to be separated from you;
From the malicious enemy defend me;
At the hour of my death call me
and bid me come to you,
that with your Saints I may praise you
for ever and ever.

O most gracious and eternal God, the helper of the helpless, the comforter of the comfortless, the hope of the afflicted, and the Saviour of all them that wait upon you; I bless and glorify your name, and adore your goodness, and delight in your love, that you have once more given me the opportunity of receiving the greatest blessing which I can receive in this world, even the Body and Blood of my Lord and Saviour. Take from me all delight in sin or vanity: let not my affections dwell below, but soar to the regions of glory, and the inheritance of Jesus: that I may love you with all my heart, and mind, and strength.

Blessed Jesus, you have exercised much love to save me, you have given your life to redeem me, your Holy Spirit to

---

1. 'Inebriate' means drunk. As someone drunk has lost all self-control, so a Christian praying this prayer wants to be under the total control of Christ.

sanctify me, yourself for my example, your word for my rule,
your grace for my guide, the fruit of your body hanging on
the tree of the cross, for the sin of my soul; and after all this,
you have sent your ministers of salvation to call me, to
holiness, and peace and happiness. My heart is desirous of
your presence, and is thirsty for your grace: as the Lord of all
my faculties, dwell with me for ever; that I may know that I
love you.

Yet Lord Jesus, you will find my heart full of cares and
worldly desires, disobedient, proud and unforgiving, false
and crafty in self-deception, full of passion and prejudice,
wicked ideas and bad habits. I know that you took our
nature, that you might suffer for my sins, to deliver me from
them, that I might serve you in holiness and righteousness, all
my days. This is my hope, my joy and my confidence.

Therefore, blessed Jesus, my Saviour and my God, whose
righteousness is my defence, priest and sacrifice of my soul,
the light of my eyes, the purifier of my stains; enter into my
heart, and cast out from it all impurities. Grant that I may
share in the holy sacrament with much reverence, receiving
your blessed body and blood, for the establishment of firm
faith, true love, and for the preservation of my body, and for
the assurance of a joyful resurrection.

*At the Eucharist, when the Bread and Wine are being
prepared:*

Holy Spirit,
Come to make us holy.
Although we cannot see you
yet you are here with us.
Make holy—our gifts of bread and wine,
   —those for whom they are being prepared,
   —those by whom they are offered,
   —and our purpose in bringing them.

May our faith be strengthened,
our love increased,
our obedience made greater.

May we with your Saints and all who have ever pleased you
share in these good things
which you have prepared for those who love you,
that in thankfulness we may
know that you live in us,
and we in you,
for whoever eats your flesh
and drinks your blood
possesses eternal life
and you will raise them up at the last day.

Before receiving Holy Communion:

Sovereign Lord
I recall before you
the saving sufferings of your Christ,
   his life-giving cross,
   precious death,
   three days' burial,
   resurrection from the dead,
   coming again.

Grant that,
   receiving the holy gifts
   I may be united to Christ;
   that receiving them in true faith and lively hope,
   Christ may live in me:
   That being made a temple of the Holy Spirit,
   I may become holy,
   understand truth,
   be strengthened against evil,
   preserved from sin,
   able to control myself.

May I keep your laws
and grow in your love within your Kingdom.

PRAYERS FOR MAKING IT UP WITH GOD

Father,
I wish I hadn't behaved like that today.
I didn't really want to
but I couldn't stop myself.

There are two sides to me,
A good side and a bad side, and today
the bad was on top.
Please forgive me,
I am truly sorry.

Help me to see my faults
and to overcome them.

Help me, too, not to lash back
when others hurt me.
Teach me to forgive them
and to treat them as friends.

It's a great relief to realise that despite our guilty consciences, God doesn't fall out with us as easily as we with him. But it sometimes feels as though he does. Is there anything that can be done? Of course.

First find a spot where you will be alone and undisturbed. A bedroom is the best place for some people. If you share one, it probably won't be.

Be quiet for a few moments and then ask the Holy Spirit in your own words to help you sort out what is unhelpful or wrong in your life, or if you're stuck use the following prayer:

Grant, Almighty God, that I may learn more and more closely to examine my life to discover my real faults. As you have given us Jesus to be our Redeemer, may I never hesitate to confess all that I find sinful. In my misery over my wrongdoing may I never be reduced to despair. I don't want to dread your presence, but rather be encouraged to approach you, my loving heavenly Father.   JOHN CALVIN

Open your Bible at Deuteronomy, chapter 5, verses 1–21 or at Matthew, chapter 5, verses 3–12 or the Letter to the Ephesians, chapter 4, verses 18–32. Read through the one you've chosen slowly and then reflect how your life measures up to the passage. If you've read the Commandments remember what Jesus told us. If we are angry without good cause we have committed murder in our hearts. Or again we may not have actually worshipped an idol, but do we put anything or anyone in the place of God? The word 'sin' comes originally from military training where it refers to an archer missing his target.

As you examine your life in the light of your passage have some paper and pencil handy so that you can write down all the failings, the near misses, that come to mind. To complete the exercise confess your sins to our Father in heaven in your own words or by using one of the confessions in your Prayer Book, or else the following prayers:

I have deceived myself dear Lord, I admit it. I have fallen from the heights to the depths. Listen to this [*now read out your list*].

I'm sorry, Lord. Lift me up again, for I know perfectly well that those only happened because I wanted them to. Save me, O save me from myself for the sake of your Son my Redeemer Jesus Christ.

ST GREGORY NAZIANZEN

I never stop going in the wrong direction, Lord, and you never stop recalling me to the right way: Grant that I may listen to your voice, accept your reproofs and submit myself to your will, through Jesus Christ our Lord.

JOHN CALVIN

Sanctify my nature, Lord, and renew me, that my heart may rise against evil, and that I may hate iniquity and every false way. Give me your power from on high to set me above the power of my sins. Turn my heart against the love of my sinful ways that I may not be false to your covenant, proving to be your faithful soldier and servant to the end of my life. Amen.

BENJAMIN JENKS

STILL GUILTY?

A very guilty conscience is sometimes a problem but the Church, inspired by the Holy Spirit, has provided a way for Christians to deal with that as well. It is known by various names: 'Penance'; 'Confession'; 'The Sacrament of Reconciliation'. You prepare for it in exactly the same way, but instead of confessing your sins by yourself you go to your minister or priest—in some churches there will be a special time for this ministry on the noticeboard. After you have confessed the priest will give you advice and then in a special prayer God's forgiveness—it is called Absolution. The one from the Book of Common Prayer *goes like this:*

Our Lord Jesus Christ, who hath left power to his church to absolve all sinners who truly repent and believe in him, of his great mercy forgive thee thine offences: and by his authority committed to me I absolve thee from all thy sins. In the Name of the Father, and of the Son and of the Holy Spirit. Amen.

You'll never believe the relief when you leave the church or your minister's study after hearing such words. And remember the person you have used as your confessor will never, never breathe a word of what you have said to anyone, not even to you.

91

After confession you might like to say the prayer which follows, or any of the prayers of thanksgiving on pages 98ff. or the prayer of St Afra on page 101.

I have been reconciled to you in Christ Jesus our Lord, and one day when I die I shall be gathered into your kingdom of eternal happiness. Show me that life is to be found even in death. I ask this through Jesus Christ our Lord.

JOHN CALVIN

PRAYER FOR MAKING IT UP WITH A FRIEND

I know an engine can't run properly
if its oil is slowly leaking away;
Eventually the car won't go at all,
until the leak has been found
and put right.

That's always such a filthy job—
the driver is tempted to put it off as long as possible.
That's fatal.

Patching up a quarrel can be messy too.
If it's not done soon it can destroy friendship.
But it's uncomfortable;
and never pleasant to make the first move.
It doesn't always come right easily and quickly,
even when the quarrel wasn't really my fault.

Lord, I want to be friends.
Help me to behave like a real friend.
Be with me, when I say sorry.
Help my friend to say sorry too.

A PRAYER WHILE PREPARING FOR EXAMS

I hate exams:
the questions don't always seem fair.
Sometimes they're too hard anyway.
I suppose we've got to have them,
but I wish we didn't.
Teachers and lecturers always say it will be all right
if we've worked!
I haven't always worked hard, but who does?
Apart from you Lord.

I don't want special favours,
but help me and my fellow students,
to do as well as we can,
and certainly as well as we deserve.

A PRAYER BEFORE STARTING SOMETHING NEW

Joining a new school,
going to a new job, is frightening.
Anything new can be.
Being on your own makes it worse.
Were you ever alone, Lord?
Did you have to visit people like dentists—
knowing what to expect, and hating it?
You were often alone on a hill,
but you wanted to be by yourself,
particularly before you had something special to do
like choosing your first Apostles.
In Gethsemane you wanted your friends with you
but they weren't much help.
What were you doing when you were alone?
Were you doing what I'm doing now—thinking things out?
Were you making sure your ideas fitted in with
your Father's?
I'd like to say to God what you did,
'Father, not what I want, but what you want.'

Cowslip (*Primula veris*)

Thanksgiving and praise

THANKSGIVING FOR HOLY COMMUNION

When you return to your place after Holy Communion:

Grant Lord that the ears which have heard the voice of your
    songs may be closed to the voice of argument or dispute:
That the eyes which have seen your great love may behold
    your blessed hope:
That the tongues which have sung your praises may speak
    the truth:
That the feet which have walked in your courts may walk in
    the regions of light:
and that the bodies which have shared in your body and
    blood may be restored to new life.
Glory be yours for your great gift.

Liturgy of Malabar

Thank you, holy Father, almighty, everlasting God who not
for any goodness of mine, but out of your own goodness and
mercy have fed me, your unworthy servant, with the precious
body and blood of your Son, Jesus Christ our Lord. May this
Holy Communion not condemn me for my sins, but bring me
salvation. Let it be armour for my faith and a shield of
goodness. May it destroy all evil desires in me, and increase
my love and my patience, defending me against all enemies
within and without, and increasing my humility and
obedience. By it may I hold to you the one true God, that one
day I may sit at your table in your kingdom. All this I
confidently ask in the name of Jesus my Saviour.

St Thomas Aquinas

After the service:

Jesus,
We have done what you asked
as well as we can.
   We have held the remembrance of your death;
   We have celebrated your resurrection;
   We are filled with your unending life
   and the joy of your eternal presence.
Good Lord, forgive everyone who has sought your guidance,
even if all that you wanted has not been done.

Lord,
I am convinced that there is nothing
   in death or life,
   in the realm of spirits or superhuman powers,
   in the world as it is or the world as it shall be,
   in the forces of the universe,
   in heights or depths,
nothing in all creation that can separate me from your love.

LANCELOT ANDREWES

Lord I bless you for calling me into fellowship with your Son, Jesus Christ, and that in this sacrament I have received the sign of his endless love. It is my highest joy that I am loved by you, for you can make me happier than I could ever imagine. Preserve me for ever in your love. By the power of the Holy Spirit keep alive in my heart the love that I feel for you at this time of Holy Communion. Again I praise and thank you for the gifts. Every day will I praise you: while I have any being I will sing praises to my God. Adored be the majesty of the eternal undivided Trinity, in whose name I was baptised and whom I humbly worship.

Blessed be your name, Father almighty, creator of heaven and earth in whom we live and move and have our being.

Blessed be your eternal Son our saviour and redeemer, the prince of peace who has purchased an eternal redemption for all.

Blessed be the Holy Spirit, the comforter who inspires me with good thoughts and holy desires to bring me to eternal life.

Possess me most merciful Father with such an appreciation of your love that I may never forget how happy I am in being so closely related to Christ Jesus. May I always count it an honour to be one of his servants that I may constantly and cheerfully obey him and delight in my calling as a Christian. In his name I ask it.

SIMON PATRICK

I bless and praise your name merciful God, that you have given me a share in the body and blood of your dear son. May this Holy Communion be comfort to my soul; health and safety to me in every temptation; joy and peace in every trouble; light and strength in every word and work; and support and defence when I come to die; through the merits of Jesus Christ our most merciful saviour and redeemer.

JEREMY TAYLOR

Good Jesus, not as I would have liked, but as I could manage, I have sought and found you. I have remembered your death; destroy in me all that is dead and give me fullness of life. I have been filled with your unending life; live in me for ever. I have received you, the true life. Forgive, dear Lord, whatever has been unpleasing. Don't let my unworthiness hinder the fullness of your blessing. Possess me completely that I may be wholly yours. Wherever I go, I bear you with me. You are not simply with me, but within me. O may I love you greatly and reverence you, and myself as well, for you have come to me. Change me to your likeness. Give me thoughts, words and acts full of you and your love, that I may be a carrier of your love.

E. B. PUSEY

GENERAL THANKSGIVINGS

Lord my God, most merciful
most secret, yet present everywhere;
most constant yet changing all things;
Never new, and never old,
Always working—always still;
creating; sustaining; perfecting all.
Who has anything except as gift from you?
What can anyone say about you?
Yet have mercy on us Lord,
that we may speak of you
and praise your name.

ST AUGUSTINE *and* JEREMY TAYLOR

Holy, holy, holy, Lord God Almighty; holy in our creation,
our redemption, our sanctification; holy in heaven, in earth,
under the earth too; holy in glorifying his angels and in
justifying his saints; holy in his glory, his mercy, and his
justice; holy in his power, his wisdom, and his providence;
holy in his ways, his laws, and his promises; holy in the
womb, in the manger, and on the cross; holy in his miracles,
his teaching, and his example; holy in his saints, and in his
sacraments; holy in himself, his Son, and his Spirit;
Therefore, with angels and archangels, and with all the
company of heaven, and all the saints in heaven and earth,
we praise and magnify your glorious name, evermore
praising you, and saying, Holy, holy, holy, Lord God of
hosts, heaven and earth are full of the majesty of your glory;
glory to you Lord most high, Lord God Almighty, which
was, and is, and is to come; glory, and honour, and thanks
be to you for ever and ever.

MARK FRANK

Glory be to the Father of mercies, Creator,
Father of our Lord Jesus Christ.
Glory be to the most holy and
eternal Son of God, our saviour and
redeemer of the world,
prince of peace and the
mighty deliverer of all who call on him.
Glory be to the holy and eternal Spirit of God, the comforter,
the sanctifying and life-giving spirit.
All glory and thanks, all honour and power,
all love and obedience
be to the blessed Trinity, one God eternally.
The heavens declare your glory,
the earth confesses your caring,
the sea reveals your power,
every spirit with every understanding creature
celebrates your greatness for ever and ever.
All glory and majesty,
all praise and dominion belong to you,
O God, Father, Son and Holy Spirit.

JEREMY TAYLOR

Transcendent God, no word can properly describe you, no
mind can fully grasp you, yet all things proclaim you and all
creation praises you. The pain and longing of the whole
world mingles about you; all things breathe you a prayer, a
silent hymn of your own composing. All that exists you
uphold; you are the end of all that is, but you are none of the
things that are. In you is the source of all light and in your
light do we see light.

Attributed to ST GREGORY NAZIANZEN

To you be praise, eternal Father; by your infinite power you made us in your image and likeness and prepared us for the everlasting possession of yourself.

To you be praise, incarnate Son. When we were lost through sin you redeemed us by your blood and opened the gates of happiness which had been shut against us.

To you be praise, Holy Spirit. You justify us by your grace and goodness, and consecrate us as holy temples to our God.

Joining with the whole creation and in union with the whole company of heaven, I adore you. Salvation to our God who sits on the throne: blessing and glory and thanksgiving and honour and power and strength be yours for ever and ever.

JOHN GOTHER

All angels and archangels, all thrones and dominions, all principalities and powers, the Cherubim with many eyes and the Seraphim covered with wings from the brightness of your glory; these and all the powers of heaven do perpetually sing praises to the glory of the eternal God, the almighty Father of men and angels. He is the immortal. Holy, holy, holy, Lord God of hosts. Heaven and earth are full of the majesty of your glory.

I also, your servant. O lover of humankind, though I am unworthy to offer praise to such a majesty, yet out of my duty offer my heart, and rejoice to join with the blessed choir and confess the glory of the Lord. You are holy. Of your greatness there is no end. O that we would therefore praise the Lord for his goodness and declare the wonders he has done for us all.

JEREMY TAYLOR

IN PRAISE OF THE CHRIST

Jesus,
a name of truth and faithfulness:
   might and power,
   majesty and glory,
   grace and mercy,
   sweetness and comfort,
   wonder and admiration,
   blessing and adoration,
to be called on by us forever that we also may be filled with:
   truth and power,
   glory and grace,
   sweetness and wonder,
and all the blessings of it:
that we may begin all
   and end all
   in you, our God and Saviour,

MARK FRANK

Jesus,
You did not come to call good people.
Your promise is clear;
it admits of no doubt.
Of your goodness you said,
that as soon as a sinner turns from evil
you would say no more about the sins.
You came to call sinners to repentance.
You offered yourself on the cross,
a victim for the salvation of the whole world.
You the innocent, for us the guilty;
You the good, for us the wicked;
You the blessed, for us the cursed;
You the sinless, for us the sinners;
To you be all praise, one God with the Father and the Holy
   Spirit,
with whom you live and reign as you always will,
age after age. Amen.

ST AFRA of *Augsburg*

I worship you Lord, I bless you most holy one,
I adore you lover of all your creation.
I give you glory, my Christ, because, alone without sin,
You gave yourself to die for me; me the unworthy.
What can I give you in return?
Glory to you for your love.
Glory to you for your mercy.
Glory to you for your patience.
Glory to you for coming as one of us.
Glory to you for your bonds.
Glory to you for receiving the lash.
Glory to you for accepting jibes and insults.
Glory to you for your crucifixion.
Glory to you for your burial.
Glory to you for your resurrection.
Glory to you that you were and are preached in the world.
Glory to you in whom we believe.
Glory to you that you were taken up into heaven.
Glory to you who sit enthroned at the right hand of the
    Father,
and will come again with his glory to judge the living and the
    dead.
When that day comes
fold your hand about me and hide me,
that I may escape to bless you for ever,
whose glorious will it is
that sinners through your mercy and compassion
should be saved.

EPHRAEM *of Edessa*

THANKSGIVING FOR SAINTS

Stained-glass windows are pretty.
The sun breaks into lots of colours as it streams through.
But surely, Lord, your saints are more exciting than that?
It's a bit hard to swallow stories about Christopher,
though medals of him, carrying you when
you were young, are good.

The story of Helena finding your cross sounds a bit far
fetched.
No-one really seems to know if there is a St George.
But Peter, Andrew and Paul, Matthew and Luke,
Alban, Catherine, Francis of Assisi and Clare,
Mary Magdalen, and your mother Mary,
are real enough.
   As your friends, they are my friends too;
And all the others, like St. . . . .
Right back to the time the Church began.
Now they are closer to you
they are much better at praising you
than I am.
   To join them, I'll use your mother's words,
'Tell out my soul the greatness of the Lord.
Rejoice my spirit in God my saviour.'

THANKGIVING FOR LIFE AND FAITH

Father, thank you. I bless and glorify you for each one of
your marvellous gifts. I thank you for having breathed into
me the breath of life, and for the preservation of my life from
day to day. I bless you for every deliverance from sickness
and suffering; for every danger averted and for every rescue
from danger. I praise you for my ability to reason, for my
sight and my speech, for my powers of movement: I bless you
for each opportunity of working for you, for myself, for all
about me. I thank you for all kindness I have received, and
for opportunities I have to be kind. I rejoice in my friends,
their affection and love; in my home and those who share it,
in those who comfort me when I am depressed or sad; in
those who cheer me up or share my excitement. I thank you
for my attacks of conscience; for the influence of the Holy
Spirit; for each victory over temptation, and each time I long
to be as good as you want me to be. All I am and all I have
are your gift to me. Let me always sing out my thanks and
rejoice in your goodness through Jesus the Lord.

C. S. VAUGHAN

Greater celandine (*Chelidonium majus*)

Prayers for others—and myself

For all Christians

Almighty God, we beseech thee graciously to behold this thy family, for which our Lord Jesus Christ was contented to be betrayed, and given up into the hands of wicked men, and to suffer death upon the cross, who now liveth and reigneth with thee and the Holy Ghost, ever one God, world without end.

Book of Common Prayer

For any community, including families

Lord, help us to live together in forgiveness.
Don't let us insist on our rights, or blame each other.
Don't let us condemn each other or find fault with each
    other.
May we accept one another as we are:
forgiving each other every day from the bottom of our hearts.

DIETRICH BONHOEFFER

For all ministries

Almighty and everlasting God, by whose Spirit the whole body of the Church is governed and sanctified: Receive our supplications and prayers, which we offer before thee for all estates of men in thy holy Church, that every member of the same, in his vocation and ministry, may truly and godly serve thee; through our Lord and Saviour Jesus Christ.

Book of Common Prayer

For parents

Lord God, preserve our families and our parents in love towards you and in health both of body and mind. Keep them from sorrow or suffering on our account and as parents care for their children, may you, Father, care for them, through Jesus Christ our Lord.

DESIDERIUS ERASMUS

For those who are unjustly accused

Lord, strengthen and support, we entreat you, all who are unjustly accused or underrated. Comfort them by the ever-present thought that you know the whole truth and will in your own good time make all things clear. Give them grace to pray for those who do them wrong. Hear and bless them when they pray through our Saviour Jesus Christ.

CHRISTINA ROSSETTI

For orphans or those from broken homes

Lord, you were rich, yet for our sakes you became poor. You promised in your Gospel that whatever is done for the least of your brothers is done for you. Give us grace to be always willing and ready to provide for the needs of those whose parents have died or whose homes are broken, that your kingdom of service and love may extend throughout the world, to your unending glory.

ST AUGUSTINE *of Hippo*

For friends and relatives

Lord, graciously accept my prayers for all my relatives and friends. Do good to them all. To those that do wrong, give grace to do better; may those that do well continue in well-doing. To those that are afflicted, give comfort and deliverance. To those that prosper, humility and temperance. Bless the sick with health, and keep the healthy from sickness. Provide for those who are in want; let those who are not in want provide for others. To all grant your grace and show your mercy. Let love bind us to one another and may our faith join us all to you. Grant that we may live and be in joy together in the bliss of heaven, through Jesus Christ our Lord.

THOMAS KEN

For special friends

O Fountain of Love, love my special friends and teach them to love you with all their hearts, that they may think and speak and do only such things as are well-pleasing to you, through Jesus Christ our Lord.

ST ANSELM

For friends

Father, by the grace of the Holy Spirit you pour gifts of love into the hearts of your faithful people, grant to those whom you have given me to love most dearly, health of body and mind, that they may love you with all their strength and happily do all that you want through Jesus Christ our Lord.

Gregorian Sacramentary

For the sick

Merciful Lord God, stretch out your hand and grant
. . . . and all nearby who are ill, the grace of
healing. Fit them for health in the name of your only Son.
May his holy name be their remedy. May it make them
sound and whole. Through Jesus, glory and power are yours
in the Holy Spirit, and yours they will continue for ever and
ever.

Adapted from the Euchologium *of Serapion*

For my country

God of all righteousness, mercy and love, give us grace and
strength to discover and do whatever may be to your honour
and glory and the good of the people of this country, that we
may become at last, through the merits of Jesus our
Redeemer, a wise, understanding and happy nation to the
praise of your name.

LORD SALISBURY

For the homeless and jobless

Father have mercy on those who are without a job or who
have no adequate shelter or home. Ensure that their needs
may be met, that faith hope and love may be rekindled in our
cities and all may be aware of their need of you, through
Jesus Christ our Lord.

ANON

For those in authority

Father in heaven, merciful and gracious, grant that those
who wield authority over others may delight in mercy and be
loving to all. Strengthen their hands and humble their hearts;
preserve them from unfair dealing or prejudice and grant
them grace always to judge in the knowledge that you are the
judge of all, through Jesus Christ our Lord.

CHRISTINA ROSSETTI

For our own needs

Give us sufficient for this life, Lord. Food and clothes; the
light of your countenance, contentment and grace to seek
first the kingdom of heaven so that we may be sure that
everything else we need will be given to us as well. Grant the
desires and hear the prayers of your servants for the sake of
Jesus Christ our Lord and only Saviour.

JEREMY TAYLOR

For truthfulness

Almighty God, you sent us the Spirit of truth to guide us to
all truth, so rule in us that we may be truthful in all we think,
what we say, and all we do. May we never lie because we are
afraid; cast out from us any inclination to take refuge in or
gain advantage by lies and bring us all into the perfect
freedom of your truth, through Jesus Christ our Lord. Amen.

B. F. WESTCOTT

The deaf

Music, Lord, tells its own story,
Exciting, vibrant; full of zest for life.
It takes me out of myself.
Sometimes it draws me to you.
Thank you for the gift of music,
for the skill and inspiration of musicians;
the delight of records and tapes;
for the rhythm of dance;
and above all for the gift of hearing.
Have mercy on those disabled by deafness
who cannot share my joy.

Sport

Lord, the training for our life in Christ is, according to Paul,
a cross between that of a soldier and an athlete.
It feels like it sometimes, especially if I'm out of condition.
When I next play in a game or watch a match
may the Holy Spirit remind me
that following your Son involves the whole of my life
and help me to train my body,
mind and spirit in the service of Jesus our Redeemer.

General intercession

I commend to your loving care and mercy,
almighty and everlasting God, all for whom I ought to pray.
You know all they need; how much do I know?
Holy Father, merciful Saviour,
gracious Spirit, one eternal God, take my
ignorant prayer; unite it to the prayer of our Lady
and all the company of heaven, and do what is necessary for
    the good
of all of those for whom I pray, through Jesus Christ our
    Lord.

ANON

The dead

Almighty Father, creator and judge of all, whose Son Jesus
Christ is the resurrection and the life, have mercy on those
who have died, especially . . . .; look with pity
on those who mourn, and at the last bring us all, living and
departed to your eternal kingdom through the same your
Son, Jesus Christ our Lord.

The dying

(This prayer is often said at the moment of death.)

Go forth upon your journey, Christian Soul!
Go from this world!
Go, in the name of God the Almighty Father who created
    you!
Go, in the name of Jesus Christ, our Lord,
Son of the living God, who bled for you!
Go, in the name of the Holy Spirit,
who strengthens you!
Go, in the name of Angels and Archangels;
In the name of thrones and dominations.
In the name of princedoms and of powers;
Of Cherubim and Seraphim, go forth!
Go, in the name of patriarchs and prophets;
Of apostles and evangelists, of martyrs and confessors;
In the name of holy monks and hermits and holy virgins,
and all the saints of God, both men and women.
Go on your course.
And may your place today be found in peace,
your dwelling in the heavenly Jerusalem:
through Christ our Lord.

A version by JOHN HENRY NEWMAN

PERSONAL PRAYERS

Another big win,
£200,000 this time.
And she doesn't know anything about football,
just picks them with the point of her knitting needle.
My dad spends hours doing his pools,
really tries to forecast each match
but he's never won very much.
What he has won only pays for the stamps, mum says.
It's not fair.
God knows, my dad's clued up on football
so he ought to win.

Why did I drag God in?
Are football pools anything to do with him?
Shouldn't think so? Yet they are part of his world.
Mountains and rivers, thunder and sunsets
are supposed to teach us about God.
Why not football pools?
They're not fair, and life's not fair.
Some people have it lucky, some don't.
Some are fit, others get things like cancer;
some win on the pools, some don't.
Life's unfair, that's a fact.
Is God responsible for that?
I don't think so, it's just what happens in life,
like winning a lot of money, or losing it.
But money's only useful if you buy things with it.
What you do with it makes all the difference.
It's not what happens that matters, but how you use it.
After all, Mary had a baby without being married,
and her Son had a cross to die on.
Yet who would have thought, Jesus,
you could use your mother and your cross
to save the world?
That's life as *you* make it, Lord.

The way you see things, Lord,
turns the world's values inside out.
According to your teaching and example:
    To serve is to be great:
    To surrender is to win:
    To die is to live:
I don't pretend to understand;
my human instincts assure me you are wrong;
but my heart tells me you're right.
Lord, by your Spirit, deepen my heart's hold on you.

Stop me, Lord God, from spoiling the fun
I know that sometimes I make
things more difficult for others than they need be.
Keep me from casting a gloom on things
by making up my mind that I am not
going to enjoy myself.
Keep me from finding a malicious delight
in criticising other people,
especially the people I live with.
Keep me from making things very
unpleasant for everyone when I don't get my own way.
Keep me from keeping all my good manners
and all my pleasantness for strangers.
Help me to try all the time to make things
easier and not harder for others, and
help me to forget my own troubles by
thinking of other people more than I think
of myself. This I ask for your love's sake.

WILLIAM BARCLAY

God grant me the serenity
to accept the things I cannot change;
the courage to change the things I can;
and the wisdom to know the difference.

Prayer used by Alcoholics Anonymous

The poverty of your birth, Jesus, shall
be my inheritance.
Your weakness as a baby, my strength.
Your rags, my riches.
Your manger, my kingdom;
all the exotic foods of the world,
but chaff to me in comparison to you;
and all the room in the world, no room
compared with that, wherever it is, where you are.
Heaven is where you are
and I will change all that I have
for your rags and manger.

MARK FRANK

Lord, I know
that one of the best ways I can show
my love for you is by loving other people.
Sometimes this is easy—
When I'm with people I like—
Please help me when loving is hard,
when people are unkind,
when they don't understand,
when I don't get my way,
when I just don't like them.

Teach me to love as you loved,
when you were walking about in Palestine—
Teach me to love as you love now—
everyone,
always.

And Lord—
When I lose my temper;
become over excited,
or get out of control;
help me to keep my feet and my fists
to myself.

Lord I ain't what I want to be;
Lord I ain't what I ought to be;
Lord I ain't what I'm going to be
but thanks Lord,
I ain't what I used to be.

ANON

O God of power, happy is the one who puts his trust in you.
By your grace I shall overcome all temptations; by your
comfort I shall be carried through all evils. Here and now
Lord I surrender myself; all that I have, or am, I give into
your hands. I leave everything to you, for you are my God.
As I thank you for your blessings, so in my troubles I will
never forget you. You want my salvation and turn everything
that happens to my good. Lord God, holy Father, your name
be blessed now and for ever.

JOHN GOTHER

Father, I enjoy giving presents;
I'm quite free with good advice too!
But I'm not sure I can give like you.
For the love of the world, you gave your Son,
in sacrifice.
Abraham was willing to give Isaac;
You surrendered Jesus;
And he, as willingly,
gave up his own life for us all.
That's what life as you see it, is about:
A willing surrender of oneself,
in your name,
and for the sake of others.
Let your Holy Spirit help me to make it.

Fronds of male fern (*Dryopteris filix-mas*)

Lord hear us

Litanies are usually offerings of public prayer and were traditionally used at penitential seasons of the Church's year. However litanies have proved over the centuries to be helpful also in private prayer. Don't rush them, and if one particular petition catches your imagination, ponder over it and don't worry if the litany you were using remains unfinished.

Litany of Christ in Glory

Glorious and forgiving king of heaven:
On your people have mercy.
You whom the cherubim praise:
On your people have mercy.
You whom the seraphim adore:
On your people have mercy.
Christ enthroned in heaven, praised by the ninefold choir of
angels:
On your people have mercy.
Christ, worshipped by the Church throughout the world, and
to whom the whole creation offers its praise:
On your people have mercy.
Christ whom the saints in glory delight to honour:
On your people have mercy.
Lord Jesus gentle son of Mary, Redeemer of the world:
On your people have mercy.
Son of God, neither made nor created but begotten of the
Father by the Holy Spirit:
On your people have mercy.
Son of Righteousness, in unclouded glory, who will come to
judge the living and the dead:
On your people have mercy.

ST DUNSTAN

Litany of the Church in the world

God, creator and author of life, warned anew of the threats
to human survival, we confess that the way we live and order
society sets us against one another, and alienates us from
your creation, exploiting as though dead, things to which
you have given life. Separated from you we live in emptiness.
Help us to struggle to conserve the earth for future
generations and free us to share together, that all may be
free.
Kyrie eleison. Lord have mercy.

God of love, who through Jesus Christ shares our suffering,
forgives our sins and delivers from the bondage of
oppression, help us to desire and nourish in ourselves
sustaining community with our brothers and sisters
everywhere. Give us courage to share our suffering when it
comes. Restore to us the joy of resurrection, that in the midst
of situations we can hardly bear we may sing out:
Hallelujah. Praise be to you Lord.

God of hope, whose Spirit gives light and power to your
people, empower us to witness to your name in all the
nations, to struggle for your own justice against all powers
and principalities, and to persevere with faith and humour in
the tasks you have given to us. Without you we are
powerless. Therefore we cry together:
Maranatha. Come Lord Jesus.

And grant that we may one with voice and one heart glorify
and sing praise to the majesty of your holy name, Father, Son
and Holy Spirit.
Amen.

World Council of Churches

Litany of the Holy Spirit

Send the Holy Spirit and by his sacred presence and almighty power may he chase from my heart, Lord:

the spirit of laxness, self-love and constant wish for an easy time;   *Amen*

the spirit of self-indulgence and sensuality;
        Amen

the spirit of pride, vanity and consuming vanity;
        Amen

the spirit of envy and squabbling;
        Amen

the spirit of hatred and spiteful talking behind someone's back;   *Amen*

the spirit of cheating, flattery and lying;
        Amen

the spirit of revenge, anger and impatience;
        Amen

the spirit of unbelief and squalid speech;
        Amen

the spirit of worrying about the unimportant;
        Amen

the spirit of coldness and lack of zeal;
        Amen

the spirit of worldliness and a disordered life;
        Amen

the spirit of carelessness and faithlessness;
        Amen

Deliver me from all the power these have had over me, that I may never more be governed nor led into sin by them, through Jesus Christ our Lord.

Spirit of truth: *guide me into all necessary and saving truths.*
Spirit of truth: *guide me to Christ.*
Spirit of truth: *guide me here and guide me hence.*
Spirit of truth: *guide me on earth and guide me to heaven.*

JOHN GOTHER *and* MARK FRANK

Litany of the Trinity

I believe, my God that you are one and there is no other God
beside you. You are the one and only true God adored by
mankind and angels. I believe, I love, I praise, I adore you,
most Holy Trinity, in whose name I was baptised and to
whose service I am committed.

   All love and all glory be yours.

All glory be yours, Father, creator of heaven and earth.
Only in you do we live and move and have our being.
Mighty wisdom, you most sweetly order, govern and guide
all things. Even our sins are used for your glory. Control my
whole life;
Steer all that I am towards the great end of our creation, to
love and glorify you.

   All love and all glory be yours.

Glory be yours, O Love enthroned in heaven. Your
resurrection and ascension are revelations of your love, for
we shall be as you are, purchased by your love. All our hopes
depend on you, for they are the trophies of your love for us.

   All love and all glory be yours.

Glory be yours, blessed and blessing Spirit of God, fire of
love which never goes out, purifying our human nature and
strengthening our weakness, shelter us under the covering of
your wings, and give us peace.

   All love and all glory be yours.

Glory be yours, Holy Trinity, for your infinite love in our
reconciliation.
Glory to you, Father, forgiving us: glory to you, Jesus, for
redeeming us;
Glory to you, Holy Spirit, purifying us. I long to be at peace
with you and praise and adore your sweet and tender mercy
that delights in forgiving sinners.

   All love and all glory be yours.

THOMAS KEN

Litany for Peace

OUR FATHER, WHO ART IN HEAVEN

We draw near to thee who hast taught us to cast all our care on thee;
Our Father, who art in heaven.
We are as children who have lost their way in the world's wilderness and we cry to thee;
Our Father, who art in heaven.
We are weak and blind and selfish; but thou art wisdom and love, and givest wisdom, love, and courage to those who trust in thee;
Our Father, who art in heaven.

HALLOWED BE THY NAME

Through the continued unity of all Christian people in allegiance to thee, overleaping the divisions caused by hostility or war;
Hallowed be thy name.
Through persistent desire in all nations to seek fellowship with one another;
Hallowed be thy name.
Through ever-deepening aspirations towards justice, goodwill, and peace in all the world;
Hallowed by thy name.

THY KINGDOM COME

By the faithfulness of thy people in seeking first thy kingdom and thy righteousness;
Thy kingdom come.
By new dedication of Christians in all lands to the establishment of justice in all the earth;
Thy kingdom come.
By the vindication of right, and by the growth of mutual understanding between nations and races;
Thy kingdom come.

THY WILL BE DONE

In the maintenance of the spirit of love and equity even in the midst of conflict;
Thy will be done.
In generous admiration for the courage and good faith of those who are opposed to one another, and readiness to believe the best;
Thy will be done.
In the determination among all to work for secure peace in a world order that is fair to the generations yet to be;
Thy will be done.

GIVE US OUR DAILY BREAD

By establishing peace, and each supplying the needs of others;
Give us our daily bread.
By co-operation among all nations and peoples for the common good;
Give us our daily bread.
By the sympathy which gives help to the needy;
Give us our daily bread.

FORGIVE US OUR TRESPASSES

Because by our self-interest and self-concern we have increased the bitterness between ideologies and between nations;
Forgive us our trespasses.
Because we have been arrogant, seeking rather to exalt ourselves, than to find thy will for us and do it;
Forgive us our trespasses.
Because we have trusted in our own wisdom and strength and have neglected thee;
Forgive us our trespasses.

WE FORGIVE THOSE WHO TRESPASS AGAINST US

If other countries, while pursuing their own interests, unduly hinder ours;
We forgive those who trespass against us.

If we have suffered loss or grief through the wrongful
ambition of others;
  We forgive those who trespass against us.
If any have injured us by threat or by attack;
  We forgive those who trespass against us.

LEAD US NOT INTO TEMPTATION

When opportunity comes to secure wealth for ourselves at
the cost of increased poverty to others;
  Lead us not into temptation.
When suffering and anxiety prompt feelings of bitterness and
hatred;
  Lead us not into temptation.
When fear distracts the mind or security lulls the conscience
and we are in danger of forgetting thee;
  Lead us not into temptation.

DELIVER US FROM EVIL

At times of self-satisfaction, self-seeking, and self-confidence;
  Deliver us from evil.
At times of boastfulness, of irritation, of despair;
  Deliver us from evil.
At times of fear concerning the designs of others and of desire
to gain security or advantage unjustly;
  Deliver us from evil.

THINE IS THE KINGDOM

For over all races and nations thou rulest as King; thy
fatherly love embraces all; and in thy will is our peace;
  *Thine is the kingdom, the power, and the glory, for ever
and ever. Amen.*

O Christ, Eternal Word of the Father, King of kings and
Lord of lords: Pour out upon all nations the gift of peace;
claim them for thine own, and make us bold to uphold thy
claim, till all acknowledge that the Most High ruleth in the

kingdom of men and that in thy service only is wisdom or joy
to be found; for thou only art worthy to receive the power
and riches and wisdom and might, who art one with the
Father and the Holy Spirit, God blessed for ever. Amen.

O God, the physician of people and of nations, the restorer
of years that have been destroyed: look upon the distractions
of the world and the divisions of thy Church, and be pleased
to stretch forth thy healing hand. Draw all unto thee and to
one another by the bands of thy love; make thy Church one,
and fill it with thy Spirit, that by thy power it may unite a
world where justice, mercy, faith, truth and freedom may
flourish, and thou mayest be ever glorified; through Jesus
Christ our Lord. Amen.

WILLIAM TEMPLE

Praise God from whom all blessings flow,
Praise him, all creatures here below;
Praise him above, ye heavenly host,
Praise Father, Son and Holy Ghost.

THOMAS KEN

Litany of Gethsemane

Jesus, in the obedience that you learned in the Garden of
Gethsemane:
Have mercy on us.
Jesus, by your courage and steadfastness tested in the
Garden:
Have mercy on us.
Jesus, in your goodness that was not embittered in the
Garden:
Have mercy on us.
Jesus, in the anguish and sorrow of those hours:
Have mercy on us.
Jesus, in your fear and trembling:
Have mercy on us.
Jesus, in the prayer that you offered in Gethsemane:
Have mercy on us.
Jesus, abandoned by the sleeping apostles,
Have mercy on us.
Jesus, who felt abandoned by God:
Have mercy on us.
Jesus, who in the Garden gave comfort to all who struggle
painfully in the agony of death:
Have mercy on use.
Jesus, whose agony in the Garden redeemed our death and
made it a happy homecoming:
Have mercy on us.
Jesus in Gethsemane:
Be merciful to us.
Jesus in Gethsemane:
Deliver us.
From ingratitude for your love:
Deliver us, Jesus.
From indifference to your suffering:
Deliver us, Jesus.
From resistance to your grace:
Deliver us, Jesus.
From doubts about God's love in moments of despair:
Deliver us, Jesus.

We poor sinners ask you:

> to teach us the depth of your surrender to the will of the Father;
> to give us your courage in the face of death;
> to teach us to watch and pray when we feel weak or discouraged.

When sorrow for our sin comes upon us:

> *Have mercy.*

When the holiness and justice of God fills us with terror:

> *Have mercy.*

When we should recognize our suffering as a share in your agony:

> *Have mercy.*

When sorrow and sadness, disgust and anguish overshadow us:

> *Have mercy.*

When we are called to share in the sufferings of your mystical body, the Church:

> *Have mercy.*

When we surrender to self-pity:

> *Have mercy.*

When our love meets hostility and ingratitude:

> *Have mercy.*

Lamb of God, you took upon yourself all our suffering:

> *Spare us, Jesus.*

Lamb of God, you redeemed and sanctified our suffering:

> *Hear us, Jesus.*

Lamb of God, who accompanies into the glory of the Father all who suffer with you and in you:

> *Have mercy on us.*

O God who hast prepared for them that love thee such good things as pass our understanding; pour into our hearts such love toward thee, that we loving thee above all things, may obtain thy promises, which exceed all that we can desire; through Jesus Christ our Lord. Amen.

KARL RAHNER
(*Collect from Book of Common Prayer*)

Night Litany

Tonight I pray Father for all who stand in most need of your merciful love and protection:

On those subject to grave temptation:
Lord, have mercy.
On those who are in deadly sin:
Lord, have mercy.
On those who in despair would turn from you for ever:
Lord, have mercy.
On those who have never sought or found you:
Lord, have mercy.
By the agony of Jesus:
Save them.
On those who are tempting others:
Lord, have mercy.
Those plotting evil or violence:
Convert by your love.
On all who are out tonight, especially young people estranged from their families; the homeless; the hungry; those contemplating suicide; those who are drunk; drug addicts:
Lord, have mercy.
By the scourging of Jesus:
Save them.
To those who work at night, especially the police; security guards; lorry drivers; politicians; firemen; railwaymen; servicemen; actors; journalists; newspaper printers; night nurses; doctors; ancillary hospital workers:
Grant them help and protection, Lord.
By the night watching of Jesus:
Save them.
On all babies born this night:
Pour your love.
On all little children, especially those in need:
Pour your love.
On the sick and suffering,
On all who are enduring any agony of mind and body:
Lord, have mercy.
All undergoing operations:

Strengthen them, Lord.
The sleepless and lonely:
Be near them, Lord.
To those in anxiety, in nervous or mental distress:
Give your peace, Lord.
To those in psychiatric hospitals:
Give your peace, Lord.
By Jesus' crown of thorns:
Deliver them.
Emergency Services called out tonight:
Go with them, Lord.
Those who this night will suffer bereavement:
Visit and sustain them, Lord.
Those who watch with the dying:
Visit and sustain them, Lord.
On all those who are dying:
Lord, have mercy.
On those who are dying alone:
Lord, have mercy.
On those dying unaware of your love:
Lord, have mercy.
On those who are afraid to die:
Lord, have mercy.
To the faithful departed:
Grant light and peace.
To those whose faith is known to you alone:
Grant light and peace.
On those who die without faith:
Lord, have mercy.
On me when I come to die:
Lord, have mercy.
By the death of Jesus:
Deliver us.

O God, whose never failing providence ordereth all things
both in heaven and earth, we humbly beseech thee to put
away from us all hurtful things, and to give us those things
which be profitable for us, through Jesus Christ our Lord.
Amen.

Community of the Sisters of the Church

Lady's mantle (*Alchemilla mollis*)

Index of subjects

Abraham and Isaac   115
Anima Christi   86
Ascension   18, 65, 121
authority   109

Baptism   55, 59, 64
before sleeping   74
before worship   1
being still   37, 44f.
Bible   2, 4ff., 23ff., 47ff.,
    67
Blessed Virgin Mary   9, 71,
    103, 110
blessings   12f.
boyfriend   107
broken homes   106
Brother Sun, Canticle of   69f.

Celtic prayers   10, 65f.
Christ
    birth of   32f.
    dedication to   35, 114
    following   9f., 40, 69, 71,
        80f.
    in glory   101, 118, 121
    prayer of   1
Christians   105
Church   1, 13, 35, 55, 59, 73,
    77, 103, 117, 126
    in the world   119
community   80, 105
confession   64f., 89ff.

country, my   108
creation   4, 30, 32, 34f., 69f.,
    99

daydreams   47
deaf   110
death   12, 21, 30, 35, 70, 111,
    128f.
dedication of self   18, 21, 27
Deer Cry   65ff.
doubt   11, 75, 126

environment   119
Eucharist   58, 83ff.
evening prayers   10ff., 74, 81,
    127
exams   92

faith, hope and love   18, 35, 39,
    74
falling asleep   74
family and friends   19f., 71,
    105ff.
food and clothes   9f., 109
football pools   112
forgiveness   5f., 9f., 32, 70, 76,
    105
frightened   74, 76, 93

Gethsemane   93, 126f.
girlfriend   107

God
  closer to   16, 20, 68
  glory of   10f., 81
  in us   17, 68, 77f.
  kingdom of   18, 81
  knowledge of   18
  longing for   4f., 30, 32
  love for   2, 16, 19, 27, 31,
      78f., 113
  love of   33, 76f.
  word of   64, 66f., 75

health   73
Heaven   12, 32, 65
holiness   11, 21, 38, 40, 60
Holy Spirit   11, 16, 35, 37f., 68,
      73, 77, 120
homeless   108
humility   18, 51
humour   73
hymns   2, 30ff.

image of God   26, 39, 68, 73,
      78f., 115
imagination   47ff.
incarnation   7, 32f.
intercession, general   110, 127

Jairus' daughter   47f.
Jesus
  at prayer   6f.
  like   19, 78f., 114
  name of   42f., 101, 108
jobless   108
Jubilate   2
judging others   78

justice   17, 106

keeping my temper   10, 114

light   11, 68
Lord's Prayer   8, 55ff., 122ff.
love for others   19, 38, 74, 114
loyalty   51f.

mantras   44
making it up   70, 92
Malabar, Liturgy of   95

meditation   47ff.
ministries   50f., 73, 105
miserable, being   16
morning prayers   2, 9, 17, 65ff.,
      71
music   110

night prayers   2, 10ff., 74, 81,
      128f.

obedience   16f., 71, 126
Office   1ff.
orphans   106
Our Father   8, 55ff., 122ff.

parents   71, 106
Passion of Christ   16, 19, 39,
      65, 67, 105, 126f.
peace   17, 70f., 80, 122ff.
penitence   12, 26, 31, 39, 77,

79, 89ff., 101
personal prayer 113f.
Peter, St 50f.
Phos hilaron 2
poems 3, 29ff., 76
praise 1, 4ff., 19, 24ff., 34f., 69f., 98ff.
prayer
  affective 44
  of adoration 19, 98ff., 121
Psalms 1f., 4ff., 41f.
purity 11, 18, 21, 40, 73

records 110
redemption 16, 24f., 38, 60, 71f., 75, 83, 102, 105, 126f.
repentance 11, 64, 89ff.
resurrection 19, 65, 67, 83, 121
revelation of God 30, 34
Ruth 51f.

St Patrick's Breastplate 65ff.
saints xif., 1, 12, 39, 41, 63ff., 84, 90, 95, 98, 101f., 106f., 118
Sanctus 25, 98, 100
self-control 20, 38, 114
self-examination 89f.
self-surrender 9, 38, 70f., 73, 79, 93, 113ff.
serving God 39, 64, 74

sex 18, 120
sick 12, 108, 128f.
sin 5, 21, 38, 40, 64, 76, 89ff., 126f.
sport 110
study 9, 93
suffering 12, 77, 126f.
Sunday prayer 83

thanksgiving for life 9ff., 19, 72, 98, 103
tongues, our 9f., 20, 38
training x, 110
Trinity 12, 64ff., 121
Trisagion 8
trust 34, 41
truthfulness 18, 109

unity 72, 77, 80, 105, 122ff.
unjustly accused 106

wandering thoughts 1, 43f.
way, truth and life 72
Weil, Simone 55
will 17, 20, 64, 68
wisdom and learning 1, 9, 17, 64, 67f., 78, 113

Zacchaeus 50

Index of selected lines

(not always first lines)

All shall be well   15
All the day long of this troublous life   12
Almighty immortal, just and merciful God   68
As a deer longs for running streams   4
Away, vain world, bewitcher of my heart   32

Batter my heart, three-personed God   31
Be still and know that I am God   44
By whose Spirit the whole body of the Church   105

Christ be with me, Christ before me   66
Continuing of the same until it be thoroughly finished   75

Dearest Lord, teach me to be generous   74

Even such is time, which takes in trust   30

Father, I abandon myself into your hands   79
Father, I enjoy giving presents   115
Father, save me from my own will   17

Give me Lord a humble, quiet, peaceable   74
Give us wisdom to know you   67
Glory be to God for dappled things   34
God be in my head   17
God grant me the serenity   113
God, I love you above everything else   27
God made the world, he loves it   15
Go forth upon your journey, Christian soul   111
Graciously to behold this thy family   105
Grant, Lord, that I may hold on to you   68
Grant, Lord, that in your wounds   19

Holy God, holy and strong   8
Holy, holy, holy   24

I believe in order that I may understand   68
I don't begin to live as I know I should   79
In the strength of God to pilot me   66
In thy word, Lord, is my trust   34

Jesus Christ, gladsome light   2
Jesus Christ, Son of God, have mercy   43
Jesus, you did not come to call good people   101

Keep us, Lord, from useless arguments   64
King of glory, king of peace   2

Let all the world in every corner sing   35
Light of the minds that know thee   64
Lord, enlighten my understanding   78
Lord, give me grace to be generous   20
Lord God, give us a steadfast faith   18
Lord God, may I be troubled by nothing   74
Lord, I ain't what I want to be   115
Lord Jesus Christ the Way   72
Lord Jesus, lift from me the misery which love of self   77
Lord, make me an instrument of your peace   70
Lord, you know how busy I shall be   17
Love bade me welcome   33

Make yourself known to us in the Breaking of the Bread   84
May I love Thee more dearly   71
My spirit longs for Thee   30

O Almighty God, who alone canst order   20
O God, who are the light of the minds   64
O God, who has prepared for them that love Thee   127
O Lord, give me a good digestion   73
O Lord, when thou givest to Thy servants   75
O Most Mighty! O Most Holy!   32
O Thou who camest from above   34f.

135

Praise God from whom all blessings flow   125
Praise God in his holiness   6
Praise the Lord O my soul   5f.

Serve thee as thou deservest   74
Since you so graciously invite us   16
Sing to the Lord a new song   4
Soul of Christ sanctify me   86
Stained-glass windows are pretty   102
Stop me, Lord, from spoiling the fun   113

Thanks be to thee, my Lord Jesus Christ   71
The poverty of your birth, Jesus   114
There is a language writt'n on earth and sky   30
The unruly wills and affections of sinful men   20

Wilt thou forgive the sin   76

You know, Father how often we sin with our tongues   20

Index of sources

Afra of Augsburg, St (martyred *c.* 303): said by some to have been a prostitute converted by a bishop fleeing from persecution. Her day is 5 August. 101

Alcuin of York (d. 804): teacher; royal tutor; Abbot of Tours in 796. 68

Andrewes, Lancelot (1555–1626): Bishop of Winchester; courtier of James I. 23ff., 56, 84ff., 96

Anselm, St (d. 1109): Archbishop of Canterbury; theologian and philosopher. 68, 107

Apostolic Constitutions: fourth-century collection of canon law, etc. 83

Astley, Sir John (1579–1652): Cavalier officer during the Civil War. 17

Augustine of Hippo, St (d. 430): greatest of the teachers of the Western Church. 12, 64, 98, 106

Barclay, William (1907–1978): Scottish Presbyterian; Professor of Divinity and Biblical Criticism, Glasgow University; popular commentator on the Bible. 113

Barth, Karl (1886–1968): Protestant theologian of enormous influence. 59f.

Becon, Thomas (*c.* 1513–1567): English Protestant Reformer; chaplain to Thomas Cranmer; fled to Continent after accession of Mary but returned under Elizabeth I. 76

Bede, The Venerable (673–735): monk who lived nearly all his life at Jarrow, where he translated and wrote commentaries on the scriptures; perhaps best remembered by his *History of the English Church and People*. 67

Benedict, St (d. *c.* 550): founder of Western monasticism. 67

Bernardine, St (d. 1444): Franciscan reformer in Italy; encouraged devotion to the name of Jesus. 39

Bessarion, Cardinal John (1400–1472): Greek scholar and very early Ecumenist. 72

Bonhoeffer, Dietrich (1908–1945): German Lutheran theologian; opposed Nazis before the Second World War and helped to found Confessing Church in Germany; imprisoned in 1942 and finally, on Hitler's orders, hanged. 80, 105

Book of Common Order: directory of worship drawn up by John Knox in 1556 for English Protestants in Geneva and used by the Church of Scotland until 1645. 75

Book of Common Prayer: service book of the Church of England, first published in 1549; the edition of 1662 still in use. 20, 41f., 91, 105, 127

Bradford, John (*c.* 1510–1555): prebendary of St Paul's Cathedral and English Protestant martyr, burned at Smithfield. 74–75

Bridget, St (d.*c.* 523): early Irish saint of great popularity; also known in England as St Bride. 39

Byrom, John (1671–1763): English poet, who wrote the well-known Christmas Hymn 'Christians Awake'. 30

Calvin, John (1509–1564): French Reformer and theologian, who lived most of his life in Geneva; wrote commentaries on many books of the Bible. 11, 12, 16f., 18, 40, 73, 89f., 92

Campion, Thomas (1567–1620): physician, poet and musician; chiefly writer and composer of songs. 34

Catherine of Siena, St (*c.* 1347–1380): Dominican; visionary; peace-maker. 72

Clare, John (1793–1864): Northamptonshire nature poet, who began writing verse while still at school. He became mentally ill by the time he was 40 and at 49 was confined in St Andrew's asylum, Northampton, where he died. 30f.

Columbanus, St (d. 615): born in Ireland; set up monasteries in England and Gaul for which he wrote a Rule; settled finally in Northern Italy. 39

de Foucauld, Charles (1858–1916): French soldier and aristocrat, who tried to found a community in the Sahara and was killed by tribesmen who suspected him of supporting the French during the First World War. His Community, Little Brothers of Jesus, eventually founded in France in 1933. 79

Donne, John (1572–1631): English poet, who was ordained and became Dean of St Paul's; a very great preacher. 31, 76

Drake, Sir Francis (1540–1596): English admiral and navigator, who helped in the defeat of the Spanish Armada and wrote the prayer given here in a letter, prior to an attack on the Spanish fleet in Cadiz harbour. 75

Dunstan, St (d. 988): Archbishop of Canterbury; adviser to the king; scholar and artist. 118

Edmund of Abingdon, St (d. 1240): Archbishop of Canterbury and friend of St Richard of Chichester. 71

Ephraem of Edessa, St (d. 373): Biblical scholar from Syria, author of many books. 102

Erasmus, Desiderius (c. 1466–1536): scholar from Holland, who supported the aims of the Reformers, but never joined their ranks; made new translation of the New Testament from the Greek into classical Latin. 72, 106

Francis of Assisi, St (c. 1181–1226): devoted to his 'Lady Poverty'; he founded an Order which is now the largest in Christendom. His deep love for God and his fellows and for the rest of creation makes him one of the most loved of the saints. 63, 68ff.

Francis Xavier, St (1506–1552): one of the early Jesuits, he preached the gospel in India and Japan. 73

Frank, Mark (1613–1664): he, with others from Cambridge, went into exile after the execution of William Laud but returned to the university at the Restoration and then held a variety of priestly offices. The prayers have all been adapted from his published sermons. 16, 19, 77f., 98, 101, 114, 120

Gother, John (d. 1704): born in Southampton of staunchly Presbyterian parents, he became a Catholic and was sent abroad by a local businessman to be trained for the priesthood. On his return he developed into an advocate of the Roman cause but also published many devotional works. 100, 115, 120

Gregorian Sacramentary: one of the early forms for the liturgy of the Church in Rome. Probably written *c*. 790. 107

Gregory the Great, St (*c*. 540–604): sometimes called the 'Father of Mediaeval Papacy'; a powerful statesman and fertile author. He dispatched St Augustine to Britain in 596. 67

Gregory Nazianzen, St (329–389): a monk and no mean theologian, contemporary and soul-mate of St Basil of Caesarea. 90, 99

Herbert, George (1593–1633): English poet and, for the last few years of his short life, parish priest at Bemerton just outside Salisbury; gentle and devout, his poems have been an inspiration to many generations. 3, 33ff.

Hilary of Poitiers, St (d. 367): engaged in the early controversies within the church concerning the nature, in philosophical terms, of the person of Christ. 64

Hopkins, Gerard Manley (1844–1889): baptised an Anglican, at twenty-two he became a Roman Catholic and two years later a Jesuit. His poems were never published in his lifetime and only began to gain their enormous popularity between the two world wars. 34

Ignatius Loyola, St (1491–1556): founder of the Jesuits, an order modelled in some respects on the kind of discipline familiar to St Ignatius in his army career and which became so powerful that it has been suppressed frequently, even by the papacy itself. 74

Jenks, Benjamin (1646–1724): son of a Shropshire vicar, he became chaplain to the Earl of Bradford and published several books of prayers. 78, 91

John of Kronstadt, St (1829–1909): a devout Orthodox parish priest on an island just outside Leningrad. His book *My Life in Christ* (1893) has proved helpful to many Christians. 41

Johnson, Dr Samuel (1709–1784): a man of letters, and famous for his English dictionary. 40

Julian of Norwich, Lady (d. *c*. 1343): an English mystic, whose cell at St Julian's Church, Norwich, is a place of prayer visited by thousands.

Her account of her visions in *Revelations of Divine Love* is a classic. 15, 38

Ken, Thomas (1637–1711): Bishop of Bath and Wells until ejected for refusing to take an oath of allegiance to King William and Queen Mary while James II was alive. He, and like-minded contemporaries, were called Non-Jurors and formed a schism from the Church of England though, unlike some of his colleagues, Ken was against any attempts to continue the break by consecrating more bishops. 19, 78, 107, 121, 125

Laud, William (1573–1645): Charles I's Archbishop of Canterbury. His attempt to impose 'decency and order' on the Church made him very unpopular among the Puritans, who eventually engineered his trial, condemnation and execution. 21, 77

Luther, Martin (1483–1546): Augustinian monk and founder of the Reformation in Germany, who left his Order as his views changed, and married. His writings influenced the English Reformers and the Church which bears his name and developed out of his teachings is now worldwide. 75

Montgomerie, Alexander (*c.* 1556–1610): Scottish poet, born on Easter Day. For a time he was courtier to the Scottish King. 32

More, Hannah (1745–1833): religious writer addressing both the wealthy classes and the uneducated poor. A friend of Joshua Reynolds and David Garrick, she had a play of hers performed at Drury Lane. In later life she lived with her sisters in the country. 9f.

More, Thomas, St (1478–1535): Henry VIII's Lord Chancellor at the time of the break from Rome, he disapproved of the King's intentions and was eventually beheaded for refusing to accept the Act of Supremacy. 73f.

Neale, John Mason (1816–1866): prodigious author and translator from Greek and Latin liturgies. He founded the sisterhood at East Grinstead: the Society of St Margaret. 16

Newman, Cardinal John Henry (1801–1890): with Pusey and Keble, a leading light in the Tractarian Movement within the Church of England, helping Anglicans to rediscover the catholicity of their Church. In 1845 he became a Roman Catholic and in 1879 the Pope made him a Cardinal. The cause for his beatification is before the appropriate bodies at the Vatican. 12, 19, 79, 111

Origen (*c.* 185–254): early and very influential biblical scholar, sometimes considered to be slightly unorthodox in his teaching. 64

Pascal, Blaise (1623–1662): French liberal theologian, mathematician and scientist; always anxious to establish religious experience rather than reason as the source of faith. 77

Patrick, St (d. *c.* 461): Apostle of Ireland, where he was first shipped as a slave when he was sixteen. Later he was ordained on the continent and returned to Ireland to preach the gospel there until his death. 63, 65ff.

Patrick, Simon (1625–1707): a Presbyterian at the start of his ministry, he sought episcopal ordination in 1654 and became, successively, Bishop of Chichester and of Ely. A prolific author, he wrote one of the first Anglican Confirmation manuals (1662). 38, 84ff., 96f.

Pusey, Edward Bouverie (1800–1882): one of the founders of the Tractarian movement, whose adherents were often called Puseyites by their detractors. He was a lecturer at Oxford for all his life and also a much sought-after spiritual director. 40, 84ff., 97

Rabbula of Edessa (d. 435): Syrian bishop and champion of orthodox teaching, who wrote many letters and hymns. 64f.

Rahner, Karl (1904–1984): son of an Austrian schoolmaster, he became a Jesuit in 1922 and was ordained while teaching theology in Holland. He was one of those appointed by John XXIII to help prepare the Second Vatican Council. 38, 81, 126f.

Raleigh, Sir Walter (*c.* 1552–1618): sailor and explorer born in Devon, he later became politically involved and was eventually executed, probably unjustly, for high treason against James I. 30

Richard of Chichester, St (*c.* 1197–1253): a faithful bishop, who while the King prevented him taking up his see at Chichester, travelled round his diocese encouraging all whom he met. He was declared a saint (canonised) just nine years after his death. 71

Roger of Taizé, Brother (b. 1915): founder and prior of the ecumenical Community at Taizé in France. 80

Rossetti, Christina (1830–1894): perhaps overshadowed by her brother, Dante Gabriel, she was nonetheless a poetess in her own right.

Her elder sister became an Anglican nun, and Christina wrote a number of religious books including a collection of prayers for every day of the year. 38, 79, 106, 109

Salisbury, Lord (1830–1903): third Marquis, Prime Minister of the United Kingdom, scientist and writer. 108

Sarum Missal: a collection of altar services for the Diocese of Salisbury, also used by many other English dioceses before the Reformation, and referred to in the *Book of Common Prayer* as the 'Salisbury Use'. 11, 20

Sarum Primer: another name for a small pre-Reformation private prayer book from the Salisbury diocese. 17

Schenute of Atripe, St (d. *c*. 450): Abbot in Egypt, who ordered a very strict Community, at one time including 2,200 monks and 1,800 nuns. 41

Serapion, St (d. *c*. 360): Bishop in Egypt, close friend of St Athanasius. Among other works he compiled a collection of prayers and liturgies which is still known as the *Euchologium* of Serapion. 108

Smart, Christopher (1722–1771): at Cambridge he got into debt and left for London and journalism. Addicted to drink and mentally unstable, he ended his days in a debtors' prison. 32f.

Solzhenitsyn, Alexander (*b*. 1918): born a year after the Russian Revolution, he became a critic of Stalin's regime and was imprisoned for a while in a labour camp. His novels describe the awful rigours suffered by those who opposed the state. Since 1974 he has lived in exile in the West. 81

Sutton, Christopher (*c*. 1556–1629): priest and devotional writer, whose book on the Holy Communion was reprinted with a fresh preface by Newman in 1838. 39

Tagore, Rabindranath (1861–1941): Indian poet, born into a wealthy family in Bengal, who also composed the music for over 3,000 of his songs. 16, 38f.

Taylor, Jeremy (1613–1667): chaplain to Charles I and supporter of the Royalist cause though he retired to Wales in 1645. After the Restoration he became Bishop in Ireland. Of his many published works, *The Rule and Exercise of Holy Living* and *The Rule and Exercise of Holy Dying* are perhaps the most famous. 18f., 21, 26, 39f., 97ff., 109

Temple, William (1881–1944): Archbishop of Canterbury, who was involved with social issues all his ministry. He proved to be no mean thinker, and was deeply affected by the two world wars of his lifetime. 17, 80, 122ff.

Teresa of Avila, St (1515–1582): with her great friend St John of the Cross, she totally reformed the Carmelite Order in their native Spain and throughout the Church. 74

Thomas Aquinas, St (1224–1274): a Dominican theologian, whose great work *Summa Theologica* is still of enormous importance to the Western Church. Not long before his death he declared to a friend that all that he had written about theology was 'as straw' when compared with the truth that he had discovered in his prayers. 84ff., 95

Vaughan, Charles John (1816–1897): first a schoolmaster; later he helped train clergymen in Doncaster and finally became Dean of Llandaff in 1879. 58f., 103

Watts, Isaac (1674–1748): Non-Conformist Minister to the Independent Chapel in Mark Lane, London and a prolific hymn writer (e.g. 'Jesus shall reign where'er the sun' and 'When I survey the wondrous Cross'). 9, 11, 57

Wesley, Charles (1707–1788): younger brother of John and a great hymn writer, the total number of whose many compositions has never been counted. 34f., 84f.

Wesley, John (1703–1791): great evangelist and founder of the Methodist Church, a man of enormous energy, who carried on a voluminous correspondence and wrote and edited a number of books while also riding about the country most of the time, preaching the gospel. He called the world his parish. 9, 17, 20, 39ff., 78

Westcott, Brooke Foss (1825–1901): schoolmaster; biblical scholar and from 1890, Bishop of Durham. 109

Wilson, Thomas (1663–1755): he initially trained for medicine, but was ordained instead in 1686; Bishop of Sodor and Man from 1698. 57f.

Wither, George (1558–1667): born in Hampshire, but settled in London to practise as a lawyer. A satirical poem landed him in the Marshalsea prison for a few months. Although he was a Royalist he remained in England during the Commonwealth and developed sympathy for the new regime. 39, 77

World Council of Churches: came into being in Amsterdam on 23 August 1948 and from time to time sets up international ecumenical conferences. 119

Bibliography

Alternative Service Book, The (1980)
Book of Common Prayer (1662)
Family Prayers (1835)
Prayers for Family Use (19th century)
Sarum Missal, translated by F. E. Warren (1911)
Andrewes, Lancelot, ed. Brother Kenneth CGA: *Private Prayers* (1974)
Barth, Karl: *Prayer and Preaching* (1964)
Calvin, John: *Commentaries* (English translation): *Daniel* (1852); Ezekiel (1844); *Jeremiah* (1850–55); *Joel* (1958)
Carmichael, Alex, and others: *Carmina Gadelica* (1928 onwards)
Fox, Selina: *Chain of Prayer Across the Ages* (1956)
Frank, Mark: *Sermons* (1849)
Gother, John: *Spiritual Works* (1740)
Hamman, Adalbert: *Early Christian Prayers* (1961)
Jenks, Benjamin: *Prayers and Offices of Devotion* (1776)
John of Kronstadt: *My Life in Christ*, by J. I. Sergieff, trans. by E. E. Goulaeff (1897)

Ken, Thomas: *Prayers for All Persons who come to the Baths for Cure* (1692)

——: *Occasional Prayers* (1708)

Ken, Thomas and Taylor, Jeremy: *Complete Manual of Family Private Devotions* (1741)

Kenneth, Brother, and Sister Geraldine: *Live and Pray* (1970)

Meyer, Kuno (ed.): *Selections from Ancient Irish Poetry* (1911)

Milner-White, Eric: *Daily Prayer* (1941)

More, Hannah: *Spirit of Prayer* (1826)

Neale, J.M.: *The Virgin's Lamp* (1868)

Newman, John Henry: *Meditations and Devotions* (1953 edition)

Patrick, Simon: *A Book for Beginners* (1662)

Pusey, Edward B.: *Private Prayers* (1882)

Rahner, Karl: *Prayers for a Lifetime* (1986)

Simpson, William and another: *Universal Prayer Book* (1759)

Tagore, Rabindranath: *Gitanjali* (1913)

Temple, William: *Manual of Prayers for War Time* (1939)

Vaughan, Charles J.: *Family Prayers and Sermon Book* (1880)

Watts, Isaac: *Duty of Prayer* (1830)

——: *First Set of Catechism Prayers* (1779)

——: *Prayers Composed for the Use and Imitation of Children* (1728)

Wesley, John: *Prayers for Children* (1828)

——: ed. J. Telford: *Letters* (1931)

Wesley, John and Charles, ed. W.E. Dutton: *Eucharistic Manual* (1880)

Westcott, Brooke F.: *Common Prayers for Family Use* (1903)

Wither, George: *Hallelujah* (1856)